European Council of International
Council of International Sc.

Effective International Schools Series

Effective Learning Support
in International Schools

Martha Haldimann
Angela Hollington

Peridot Press

Published 2004 by Peridot Press,
a division of John Catt Educational Ltd
Great Glemham, Saxmundham, Suffolk IP17 2DH, UK
Tel: +44 (0) 1728 663668 Fax: +44 (0) 1728 663415
E–mail: info@peridot.co.uk Internet: www.peridot.co.uk

Opinions expressed in this publication are those of the contributors, and are not
necessarily those of the publishers or the sponsors. We cannot accept responsibility
for any errors or omissions.

The Sex Discrimination Act 1975. The publishers have taken all reasonable steps to
avoid a contravention of Section 38 of the Sex Discrimination Act 1975. However,
it should be noted that (save where there is an express provision to the contrary)
where words have been used which denote the masculine gender only, they shall,
pursuant and subject to the said Act, for the purpose of this publication, be deemed
to include the feminine gender and vice versa.

A CIP catalogue record for this book is available from the British Library.

ISBN: 1 904724 02 7

Designed and typeset by Peridot Press, a division of John Catt Educational Limited,
Great Glemham, Saxmundham, Suffolk IP17 2DH, UK

Printed and bound in Great Britain by Bell and Bain Ltd, Glasgow, Scotland.

Dedication

To all the children who slipped through the net and to all those who didn't.

and

To that elusive normal child... We hope we never find you.

Contents

Appendices

Foreword: Effective International Schools Series

ECIS/CIS are not-for-profit organisations dedicated to the advancement of internationalism through education by the provision of services to their members.

ECIS/CIS member schools are spread around the globe and are immensely varied in nature. Yet any of them, new or established, large or small, day or boarding, co-educational or single sex, monocultural or multicultural, can aspire to developing internationally-minded students. The sole proviso, as expressed in the ECIS Statement of Philosophy, is that they are committed to the promotion of an international outlook amongst all members of their communities.

ECIS and CIS see their roles as providing services, which actively assist schools in working towards this ideal, through practical support. The Effective International Schools series is one way of doing this.

For the purposes of this series, ECIS/CIS will restrict themselves to those areas of a school's operation with regard to which the Councils are in a position to offer sound practical support in the form of documents which offer reliable guidelines and proven examples of good practice. There is much to be gained from sharing the experiences of member schools and little to be gained from reinventing the wheel. Much has been learned since ECIS was founded and time, energy and money are too precious to waste. The experience of other schools may offer a real head start.

Each publication will, therefore, have the following elements in common:

- They are driven by a common set of beliefs and values about student learning with an international outlook;
- They are structured so as to illustrate a logical progression from profile to policy to practice;
- They are based on successful experience in international schools, but offer suggestions generic enough to apply in a variety of contexts.

ECIS and CIS trust this series will prove useful to members and welcome any suggestions for improvements to each publication or for additions to the series.

Kevin Bartlett is Director of
the International School of Brussels, Belgium

Commentary

Effective Learning Support in international schools is now an expectation of parents and the accreditation agencies. The levels of support available will always be very different from school to school depending upon local conditions. That being said there is a basic minimum that we have to provide. Further, if we are going to offer the exceptional educational opportunities that many of us describe in our mission statements then we have to go well beyond the basics.

Many school heads in my position are isolated from our national systems and find it increasingly difficult to come to terms with what we should be doing in our schools. We see more and more needs for student support but are limited in finding the advice that we would require in order to make a reasoned judgment about how to best help the situation. In order to be aware of the practicalities of how to offer good support we rely on a Special Needs teacher coming from one background or another; very few have long experience in international schools. We finish up with programmes that skew one way and then another with good practice being lost with changes of personnel.

I feel very fortunate to have worked with Martha Haldimann in my school for six years and continuing to work with her from a distance for a total of ten years. In this book she and Angela Hollington manage to put together years of experience in the international school environment about what to do and why we should do it. For a school that is unsure about what special needs are and how they should be addressed this is essential reading. For a school that thinks that it is doing a good job it is also essential reading if we want to truly reach out to our missions and philosophies.

David Gatley
Director, International School of Stuttgart.

Introduction

We would like to thank ECIS/CIS and Mike Maybury for giving us the opportunity to meet each other, discuss, debate and write about the fascinating area of learning differences. Also, thank you to Ann Pönisch, Jennifer Henley and Peridot Press for their editing, e-mails and telephone calls and to the mystery editor wherever you are.

However, our very special thanks go to Christopher Fox, an 11-year-old student in the International School of Geneva (Pregny-Rigot), who drew the cartoons to illustrate certain chapters. He was an inspiration to us in the writing of the book and made us both realise how a 'Special Need' is really a relative concept.

Thank you, Christopher.

Preface

Why are we writing this book anyway?

It is not acceptable for international schools to state that they will not enrol children with special needs, since by definition all international children have Special Needs. However, within an international school there are certain groups of students, *eg* ESL, learning disabled, gifted, with additional educational needs who require instruction beyond what the regular classroom curriculum can provide. Children with Special Educational Needs are no longer 'exceptions' at international schools. We believe that it is unethical for international schools to accept students with special learning needs and not provide accommodation for their needs within the classroom environment and/or within a Learning Resource Centre at the school. All students at international schools should be expected to succeed whether or not they require additional support to meet their educational needs. It is recognised that this book does not fully address the specific requirements of ESL students and those ESL students who may have additional learning needs. The complex and important issue of ESL students with specific learning needs has not been covered in this book as it could be dealt with in another book entirely devoted to this group of students. However, if heads of schools and school staff were provided with adequate information about types of learning needs seen at international schools, an ESL student presenting some type of special learning need might be detected earlier.

The nature of special needs is constantly changing and we as educators need to adapt to these changes. Flexibility and adjustment are part of an international school's daily life as these schools have to deal with many issues, *eg* cross-cultural differences, multitude of mother tongue languages, cultural clashes between students/parents/staff, objective assessment and accommodation of children from many different counties. The aim in writing this book is to give heads of schools a practical guide to how to meet the needs of children who require more support in order for them to reach their potential. It is our opinion that heads need to be aware of all facets of a learning support programme to communicate with different groups within the international school community and to lead the staff in accommodating special needs students in the classroom and/or in a Learning Resource Centre. *Effective Learning Support in International Schools* is a book that heads can share with all members of the school community in order for the international school to provide a consistent approach in allowing all children to succeed.

To address the issue of effective learning support in international schools, the Optimal Match model has been selected as a philosophy of education as one way in which to incorporate the needs of all children. The Optimal Match model is an approach whereby all students receive the 'best fit' of the curricula to the student rather than a 'one size fits all' approach. Children with special learning needs are given the specific support they require in order for them to be successful and help them achieve their maximum potential. The extent to which this can be implemented is obviously a budgetary consideration and may be dependent on the discretion of the head or the board of the school. However, if we are to be truly international and accept children from all parts of the globe, we are already accepting children with different needs. Therefore accepting children with specific learning needs at international schools is inevitable.

Our role as international educators is to value differences and create school environments where different student needs are accommodated.

As Forrest Gump asks: "What does normal mean anyway?".

Chapter One

What are Special Needs?
What are we talking about?

The nature and definition of special needs are sensitive issues. Sensitive not only with parents (no child of mine has a special need!), but also with teachers who might feel inadequate in providing everything that each child needs within the classroom. Certainly an international school, by definition, has students who, in any national system, might be identified as having special needs that might require additional learning support.

In a random survey of eight elementary classes at three international schools, the following data were recorded:

Table to show range of needs within a sample of eight classes at three international schools

Grade level	Total # students	# ESL students	# diagnosed with LD	# with emotional difficulties	# gifted & talented
1	24	9	0	0	1
1	21	14	2	0	1
2	25	10	3	1	0
3	25	8	1	2	1
4	25	7	3	3	3
4	25	3	5	4	8
5	25	4	4	1	1
6	22	9	2	2	2

The table shows that one could find from 20 to 50 percent of children with special learning needs in the regular classroom including ESL students with special additional learning needs. Many children entering a new international school might be experiencing culture shock and/or language shock having moved from another country. In other cases, many children who have moved country and changed schools may just have missed the essential lessons, which make a difference to the child's understanding of a concept. Teachers need to be very aware that a student's previous education and emotional experiences have immense bearing on a child's performance at an international school, as does parental influence. Therefore, heads and teachers need to be sensitive and observant to incoming students who may be showing a temporary special learning need which will pass when the student has been fully integrated into the school. Contrarily, children who are just at the beginning stage of learning English, especially young children, may be in need of special needs support but does not show it due to the difficulties of learning English. In the first *International Schools Journal Compendium: Culture and the International School* (Peridot Press, 2003), there is a whole chapter devoted to the question, 'Is it a language problem or a learning disability?' (conversation with Edna Murphy, Editor of the *ISJ Compendium*, June 21, 2003). The section contains many articles about language learning and learning difficulties. When looking at the whole concept of special needs, the parents' needs should also be catered for. This subject will be dealt with in more detail in Chapter 7, *The role of the school to parents,* but it needs to be stated that when looking at effective learning support, one should look at the whole family and not just the individual child.

Rationale

Special Needs/Learning Support – an Optimal Match approach

The authors believe that one approach to address the needs of all students at international schools is to incorporate a philosophical/educational model – the Optimal Match Concept. This is 'both a philosophy of education and the fine-tuning of curricula to match an individual student's demonstrated level and ideal pace of learning' (CTY, 1994). With Optimal Match, student learning is based on identifying the zones of appropriate challenge, which relate closely to Vygotsky's zone of proximal development (Daniels, 1996) and providing instruction for students to work in those zones. Assessment of achievement and abilities, both formal and informal, is considered to be the first step to achieving an appropriate curricular match. The learning needs of students, who are ESL speakers, are learning disabled, or who exhibit exceptionally high abilities or talents are specifically targeted, as well as the learning needs of the school's general population (Advisory Committee on Exceptional Children and Youth, ACECY, 1993).

The essential elements of the Optimal Match model are:

- a respect for the sense of uniqueness and worth of human individuality, of difference rather than disability;

- a sense of development, of process, of growth, of change in individuals;

- a recognition that all individuals differ and that when these differences are dealt with positively, students will be able to develop their full potential and capitalise upon their own abilities and styles;

- for individuals with special needs because of a mismatch of what they bring to a situation and what is expected, an active partnership between school, home, community and student is even more critical than it is for other students; and

- the belief that through skilled and sensitive teaching and support, students with differing abilities and talents can find individual paths to success and fulfilment and can contribute to the fulfilment of other students.

(Advisory Committee on Exceptional Children and Youth,
ACECY/IAAY, 1997).

The Optimal Match Concept is not new; it was conceived in 1986 and has been practised at international schools throughout the world. An excellent example of putting philosophy into practice is explained in the recent publication, *Count Me In!* (Kusuma-Powell & Powell, 2000). The book has been written by international educators for international schools and is rich in resources for teachers. Although the term Optimal Match Concept is only specifically mentioned in the chapter, *Teaching Exceptional Children,* under the heading of *An Educational Approach For Teaching Highly Capable/Gifted Students,* the concept is reflected throughout the book as a type of inclusion approach to meet the needs of all the students at international schools. Essentially, Optimal Match practices at international schools represent 'good teaching' for all students in the general international population with a special emphasis on students who are in need of special educational support: the ESL students, students with high academic abilities and talents, students with specific learning disabilities, and any other Special Needs students who present themselves with exceptionalities.

To further illustrate the practice of Optimal Match at international schools, the 'Discussion' section has been taken from *Special Learning Needs in International Schools: The Optimal Match Concept* (Haldimann, 1998) and is quoted below:

'Collaboration, commitment, and communication are common themes reflecting Optimal Match principles at the four international schools quoted. Elsa Lamb at the American School of Barcelona wrote of her school's student study team approach and checklist, which emphasises these themes. Annette Nyqvist described the type of accommodations, extensions and programmes in place at the International School Manila. These practices reflect the school's commitment to meeting their student learning needs. Cynthia Silva at the Graded School, São Paulo, wrote extensively of the comprehensive Optimal Match practised at her school. Graded has incorporated the Optimal Match model philosophy and approaches at all grade levels, and the Optimal Match approach is included in the school's mission statement.

'This is an important point. The ACECY (Advisory Committee on Exceptional Children and Youth) conducted a survey of Optimal Match practices at international schools world-wide (Durden, 1996). The most important finding from the survey was the recommendation that international schools should emphasise their commitment to the Optimal Match to the school community by placing Optimal Match approaches in the school's mission, aims, and objectives statements. David Gatley at the International School of Berne clearly states that there must be a school, staff and parent commitment to the Optimal Match process, and cautions against promising more than the school can offer. He emphasises the importance of communication of all parties involved with the individual student and brings the reader's attention back to redressing the balance of education to the individual student through the Optimal Match philosophy.'

The descriptions of Optimal Match practices at four international schools illustrate the diversity of student learning styles and profiles. This calls for adapting the curricula to the student rather than the student being instructed to a fixed curricula. This is central to the Optimal Match Concept contrary to a K-12 curriculum where one size fits all. Maria de la Luz Reyes (1992) alludes to an Optimal Match or best fit and challenges the assumption that one style fits all without modifications. She refers to the fallacy of 'the assumption that instruction which is effective for mainstream students will benefit all students, no matter what their backgrounds may be'.

Accurate assessment, both formal and informal, is thus an essential component to the Optimal Match. Standardised testing is strongly advocated (Mills and Durden, 1996) at international schools for students with mother-tongue English, ESL students whose level of English permits taking these tests, and students with learning difficulties, allowing test-taking accommodations when necessary. Not only are standardised tests one method for identifying academically talented students, the tests also provide a measure of English language development for ESL students over time. International students tend to move frequently, and these tests provide an objective measure of basic achievement and abilities where there may be different methods and levels of instruction from school to school where children by relocation may have gaps in their learning. Informal or teacher-made tests may be applicable to one specific school but not to another; therefore, standardised tests may provide the only common basis for measuring student abilities and achievements over time.

There are many concerns among international school teachers that ESL students should not be administered group standardised tests because the US or British tests most commonly used are culturally biased; therefore not appropriate for ESL students. However, realistically speaking, ESL students are bombarded daily with all types of cultural biases that it becomes normal for these students. Usually international school curricula are eclectic, *eg* a British maths scheme, an American reading scheme. Teachers from many different countries at an international school speak English with their own accents, and students are exposed daily, for example, to CD-ROMs, videos, music, MTV, CNN, BBC, the Internet – all in English. The cultural bias argument about standardised testing does not make much sense. Please refer to the Mills and Durden article about standardised testing at international schools in the Appendix C, *Handouts*.

One theme running through the descriptions of Optimal Match practices is flexibility. It is well known that, at many international schools, English mother-tongue students are in the minority and teachers are essentially ESL teachers (Bartlett, 1995); flexibility in teaching styles is a necessity. International school students move in and out of schools frequently, sometimes during the school year, and it is common for a grade to start the year with a set student roster and complete the school year with a 30-40 percent turnover. This fact leads heads of schools to help teachers develop sensitivity to assessing and matching curricula for their students, especially students with special learning needs, by in-service training, attending workshops, and conferences.

In summary, Durden and Mills (1996) write: 'The value of the Optimal Match is most apparent when it is applied to students with obvious special needs – as in the case of highly able children or those with learning disabilities.

But focus on these groups only illuminates the applicability of the concept for all children.' Indeed, in thinking about the relevance of the Optimal Match, we might recall the words of the seventeenth century physician William Henry: 'Nature is nowhere accustomed more openly to display her secret mysteries than in cases where she shows traces of her workings apart from the beaten path'.

Parallel to the Optimal Match model, the Council of International Schools (previously the European Council of International Schools) June 2003 Seventh Edition Standards and Indicators from the *Guide to School Evaluation and Accreditation* closely follow the Optimal Match model with its inclusion of specific guidelines for identification and accommodation of special needs students in *Section E: Student Support Services*. For example, indicators related to accreditation standards clearly state:

- There shall be effective procedures for identifying the learning needs of students, both at admission and thereafter.

- If children with learning or other disabilities or remedial needs are admitted, the school shall provide specific curricula and programmes to meet those needs.

- The school shall have the trained special needs personnel needed to serve students with identified learning disabilities.

- There shall be effective practices to address the needs of students of exceptionally high ability, achievement, and/or talent.

- If students whose native or first language is not English (and whose English is not sufficiently developed to follow the full school curriculum) are admitted, the school shall provide English Language Support/ELS.

- The school shall provide appropriate guidance services, including academic and personal counselling as well as career/tertiary education advice, for secondary students.

- The school shall work cooperatively with parents and keep them informed of the academic and social development and progress of their children.

- The school shall provide opportunities for students to take all appropriate tests, including those for admission to institutions of higher education, and shall assist parents and students in processing required application materials.

- The school shall provide adequate health care, and shall insure provisions for emergencies on-site and at school functions which take place away from the school premises.

- The school shall have health policies, which include collection of medical information for all staff and students, immunisation against common diseases and the maintenance of comprehensive records.

(Gerry Percy, July 10, 2003, CIS/NEASC Standards and Indicators from the *Guide to School Evaluation and Accreditation*, Seventh Edition).

The CIS/NEASC Accreditation Guidelines also provide a rating system for specific functions of all aspects of Student Support Services. Similar statements are also to be found in *Count Me In!* (Kusuma-Powell & Powell, 2000) where the idea of inclusion for an international school means that all students are provided for and none are excluded from instruction. If a head of an international school were to set up a special needs programme using *Effective Learning Support in International Schools* as a guide to support services, it would basically meet the CIS/NEASC Student Support Services guidelines. It is recommended to obtain a copy of the CIS/NEASC Standards and Indicators from the *Guide to School Evaluation and Accreditation* even if the school were not involved in the accreditation process. With the three documents, *Effective Learning Support in International Schools, Count Me In!* and the CIS/NEASC Standards, an international school would be able to start to develop or enhance a Special Needs/ Learning Support programme.

Chapter Two

Developing a Special Needs/Learning Support programme
Don't we all have special needs?

The development of a Learning Resource Centre (LRC) is recommended whether in a school of 60 students or a school of 1,500 students. The functions of the LRC would be to identify students requiring learning support and to recommend the type of learning support that students might receive. This means that a student might be seen at the LRC for a certain number of periods per week and/or the LRC teachers might work with that student in the regular classroom. Another function of the LRC teachers would be to advise the regular classroom teacher on how to adapt the curriculum to student needs in the classroom. The criteria for introducing the Optimal Match Model plus the CIS accreditation guidelines can provide enough information for a school to begin to develop a Special Needs/Learning Support programme. However, it is important to consider all aspects of what is involved *before* starting up such a programme and to establish staff consensus regarding Special Needs and how developing a Special Needs/Learning Support programme will impact on the regular classroom teachers.

It is recommended to create a Special Needs development committee, which includes the head of school and members of the different school sections. In this way, input from the entire school staff can be assimilated to develop a Special Needs/Learning Support programme. One international school head placed a questionnaire in each of the teachers' mailboxes, with the question 'Why Learning Support?' written at the top of the page. The head and Special Needs Development Committee asked for comments on the questionnaire and to be returned to the committee within one week.

These are some of the comments the teachers wrote:

- to help me as a teacher;
- to develop skills and provide support for the student's weakest area;
- to stimulate students who demonstrates special talent or high ability;
- to honour a student's individual learning needs and develop his/her potential to the fullest;
- to reduce disruptive behaviour in the classroom;
- to produce successes rather than failures;
- to assure a minimum standard of performance for every student;
- to create a whole and trusting atmosphere for the learning disabled student;
- to allay parents' fears that no programme exists;
- to support the student in succeeding in the mainstream classroom.

Schools might want to use this procedure as an introduction to an in-service workshop as one of the first steps to developing a special needs/learning support programme.

After presenting a strong argument for the development of a Special Needs/Learning Support programme, it is recommended that the Development Committee address the following six key areas before announcing the creation of such a programme:

Requirements for a Special Needs/Learning Support programme

1. Policies

   - Statements regarding students with Special Needs in the school's policy manual and in the school's brochure.

   - Enrolment criteria.

   - What type of Special Needs student can we realistically accommodate?

2. Organisation, services and personnel

   - How do we organise the school to accommodate students with Special Needs?

   - What kind of services can we provide?

   - Who will provide them?

3. Assessment and identification

   - What type of assessment do we need?

   - How are the students referred for assessment?

   - Once identified, what are we going to provide for the student?

4. Programme delivery and accountability

   - What type of programme can the school deliver to children with Special Needs?

   - How do we evaluate whether or not the programme is effective?

5. The parent – school relationship

   - What support can we provide to the parents of children with Special Needs?

6. Evaluation

   - How can we evaluate the effectiveness of the Special Needs provision in our school?

   - Who will evaluate the Learning Resource Centre staff? And with what criteria?

   - Should the LRC be required to produce an LRC policy and curriculum guide for evaluation of LRC functions?

The Optimal Match model advocates meeting the needs of the student by fine tuning and adapting the curriculum to the child. However, the extent to which this can be realistically achieved is dependent upon the resources available and the commitment of the entire faculty to providing the best possible education for each child in the school.

Definitions

Every child is different, and every child has different learning needs. Learning needs may be categorised using different criteria, and it must be stressed that these definitions are not all mutually exclusive. It should be repeated that teachers should be looking at the whole child and their learning needs. We have placed certain definitions under categories in order to address the major groups of children with special learning needs, which are the most common at international schools. It is recognised that ESL students may also have special learning needs besides learning English to which these definitions may apply.

Gifted and talented

Feldhusen, Van Tassel-Baska & Seeley (1989), wrote in their introduction section, 'What is the Historical Background of the Gifted Movement?', that the research of Lewis Terman and his colleagues, which started in 1921 with individuals identified with IQs greater than 140, paved the way for the beginning of the gifted and talented movement within the United States. Although studies continued through the following years it was only until 1969 that the US Congress authorised the US Commissioner of Education to conduct a study on the status of the educational services for the gifted and talented at schools in the United States. That study was published in 1972 as the Marland Report. The study had a tremendous effect in establishing the following definition of gifted and talented:

'Gifted and talented children are those identified by professionally *qualified* persons who by virtue of outstanding abilities are capable of high performance. These are children who require differentiated educational programs and services beyond those normally provided by the regular school program in order to realise their contribution to self and society.'

Children capable of high performance include those with demonstrated achievement and/or potential ability in any of the following areas:

1. General intellectual ability;

2. Specific academic aptitude;

3. Creative or productive thinking;

4. Leadership ability;

5. Visual and performing arts;

6. Psychomotor ability.

(Marland 1972, p2)

Thus, the older monolithic view of giftedness simply as high intelligence began to be displaced in favour of a multi-faceted view of talents and abilities. That view would later be extended and modified in a seminal and influential theoretical analysis of giftedness by Joseph Renzulli in 1978. 'This latter work extended the conception of giftedness to motivational aspects and creativity' (Feldhusen, Van Tassel-Baska, Seeley, 1989). The definitions remain mostly the same to this day and are generally accepted worldwide. Within these six areas, there are different approaches, which propose to identify students who are gifted and talented (*eg* Gardner, Sternberg), but for international school students, who often do not speak English, a case-by-case approach to the identification process is necessary.

A seventh area is proposed here – that of computer expertise. The Marland definitions have held up over time as is described in the 1987 US Federal Javits Gifted and Talented Act and the 1993 US Office of Educational Research and Improvement document: 'Children and youth with outstanding talent perform or show the potential for performing at remarkably high levels of accomplishment when compared with others of their age, experience, or environment' and 'These children and youth exhibit high performance capability in intellectual, creative, and/or artistic areas, possess an unusual leadership capacity, or excel in specific academic fields. They require services or activities not ordinarily provided by the schools'.

A new approach to the identification of the gifted is a description of giftedness expressed as developing expertise as was described by Robert Sternberg in *High Ability Studies*, The Journal of the European Council for High Ability. Robert Sternberg's (Sternberg, 2001). Sternberg, in his article 'Giftedness as Developing Expertise: a theory of the interface between high abilities and achieved excellence' proposes a developing expertise model containing six general specifics:

- metacognitive skills;
- learning skills;
- thinking skills;
- knowledge;
- motivation;
- context.

The developing expertise model shows the interactions of these areas and relates these areas to the 'novice' moving through the specifics to developing expertise as they become the 'expert'. Dr Sternberg describes three aspects of giftedness as developing expertise:

- analytical;
- creative;
- practical.

He further suggests that these areas are necessary for success in life and emphasises that school success may not necessarily mean success with these three aspects of giftedness which are necessary for success in life. His table 'Comparison of static, dynamic, and develop-expertise views of giftedness' is an eye-opener. In the opinion of the authors this developing expertise model might become the model of the future and international schools may wish to explore it further.

Although the label of 'gifted and talented' is used often, a more descriptive label is 'an individual with high potential in certain areas'. Enrichment programmes should be offered to encourage this potential and not created to place all students with high potential into one programme. It is common for individuals to state that a student has a high IQ or an IQ of 140; these statements are only part of the picture. More information about the student should be requested rather than accepting a global score.

The manual for the Wechsler Intelligence Scale for Children-III states:

'Definitions of giftedness typically mention the potential for unusually high performance in several areas besides the intellectual domain. Thus, an evaluation of a child for possible giftedness will normally include assessment not only of intellectual ability but also of other skills and talents. Furthermore, because the definition of giftedness will vary from setting to setting, and from one program for the gifted to another, the examiner may need to design different assessment procedures for different situations'

(Wechsler,199, p9).

If *only* a global IQ score were given to parents and teachers, then all the information from the Wechsler tests – Verbal and Performance test scores and the various subtest scaled scores – should be requested. From those sixteen scores from the Wechsler Intelligent Scale for Children (WISC III), for example, valuable information can be obtained and a learning profile and an IEP for the student can be constructed. The WISC-III profile form on page 80 could be sent to the parents or psychologist to complete. If a complete testing report has been received, the scores can be transferred to the form to act as a common means for communicating to parents who usually are not given adequate information as to the nature of their child's intellectual profile. This should be the case whenever the Wechsler tests are administered to students which special learning needs. Teachers and parents of students with learning disabilities also need to have access to complete Wechsler profiles in order to see their child's intellectual strengths as well as weaknesses.

Many gifted and talented programmes or support given to a gifted student have some type of a cut-off IQ point for entrance into the programme or to be identified as intellectually gifted (*eg* IQ 125 – upper 5% of the general population, IQ 130 – upper 2% of the general population, either in the Verbal or Performance domains or Full Scale IQ). This means that if these numbers were used at international schools (for example, at a school of 250 students) 5% of the student population could probably be identified as gifted and talented, or about 12 to 13 gifted children.

Demystifying some commonly held stereotypes about children with high potential and talents.

These students do *not* necessarily:

- show high potential in everything (as seen above, they can have high potential in different areas or in one area only);
- succeed in school without any intervention (from 20% to 50% of these children may have problems in school) (Adda, A, 1999 and Terrassier, J-C, 1998);
- stand out in the classroom (often they try to hide their intelligence to be able to fit in with their peers);
- be easily identified (research has shown over and over again that teachers are the least likely to identify children with high potential);
- behave well (sometimes their hypersensitivity or boredom creates behavioural problems);
- show pride in their high potential and talents (usually they try to hide their high abilities in order not to stand out and may worry about why they are different from their peers);
- feel happy (they become bored easily, become frustrated if not challenged and can become depressed);
- have 'pushy' parents (their parents often need support and advice on how to respond to their child's questions which are often more complex than for the average child).

Dr William G Durden, former Director of the Institute for the Academic Advancement of Youth, The Johns Hopkins University (renamed CTY), presented the following important factors for talent development in children during his lecture at the 1995 Optimal Match Network Institute-OMNI (see *Appendix E, Resources* for OMNI coordinates):

- early and ongoing parental support and intellectual stimulation;
- early commitment of children by intense and continuous work in a specific field;
- a flexible educational environment with opportunities for individualised pacing and continued challenge;
- teachers who serve as role models and mentors, setting high standards, modelling and transmitting values as well as information;
- opportunities for interaction with a peer group of similar interests and abilities.

The following comes from the website of the National Association for Gifted Children (USA). Heads of international schools can use these questions and answers when confronted with parents, staff and/or board members about the need to provide gifted education to the school's gifted students.

Why should gifted education be supported?

This question is often asked in a confrontational manner by those who believe that gifted individuals do not need special educational provisions. Some sincerely feel that truly gifted children will remain gifted and fulfil their educational needs on their own. Others feel that if teachers are doing their job, the gifted should be able to get by without the special attention that other atypical learners need. The following are some ideas that those who hold such views must be asked to consider:

1. Gifted learners must be given stimulating educational experiences appropriate to their ability if they are to realise their potential. Giftedness arises from an interaction between innate capabilities and an environment that challenges and stimulates to bring forth high levels of ability and talent. These challenges must be available throughout the individual's lifetime for high levels of actualisation of ability and talent to result. According to research on the nature of intelligence and the brain, we either progress or we regress depending on our participation in stimulation appropriate to our level of development.

2. Each person has the right to learn and to be provided with challenges for learning at the most appropriate level where growth proceeds most effectively. Our political and social system is based on democratic principles. The school as an extension of those principles must provide an equal educational opportunity for all children to develop to their fullest potential. This means allowing gifted students the opportunity to learn at their level of development. For truly equal opportunity, a variety of learning experiences must be available at many levels.

3. At present, only slightly over one-half of the possible gifted learners in the United States are reported to be receiving education appropriate to their needs. There is physical and psychological pain in being thwarted, discouraged and diminished as a person. To have ability, to feel power you are never allowed to use, can become traumatic. Many researchers consider the gifted as the largest group of underachievers in education.

4. Traditional education currently does not sufficiently value bright minds. Gifted children often enter school having already developed many of their basic skills. Almost from the first day they sense isolation, as others consider them different. Schools are not sufficiently individualised or flexible to allow modification in structure and organisation. Most schools seek to develop skills that allow participation in society, not the re-creation of that society.

5. When given the opportunity gifted students can use their vast amount of knowledge to serve as a background for unlimited learning. When the needs of the gifted are considered and the educational programme is designed to meet their needs, these students make significant gains in achievement, and their sense of competence and well-being is enhanced.

6. Providing for our finest minds allows both individual and societal needs to be met. Contributions to society in all areas of human endeavour come

in overweighed proportions from this population of individuals. Society needs the gifted adult to play a far more demanding and innovative role than that required of the more typical learner. We need integrated, highly functioning persons to carry out those tasks that will lead all of us to a satisfying, fulfilling future.

http://www.nagc.org/ParentInfo/index.html#Why.
(National Association for Gifted Children. June 13, 2002)

It is recommended that schools purchase some of the books written about gifted/talented students cited in Appendix E, *Resources*. These books could be loaned by the LRC to parents and teachers. It is surprising how many teachers hold stereotypes about the gifted and talented and fail to understand their needs. A teacher was once overheard to say to such a student, "If you are so gifted, why don't you show it?" Needless to say this teacher was uninformed about high potential and talents.

Learning disabilities

In 1975, the US Office of Education published Public Law 94-142 The Education of All Handicapped Children Act. Among various definitions, the Office published a definition of learning disabilities. This definition has remained basically unchanged in the 1998 The Individuals with Disabilities Act (IDEA) replacing the Public Law 94-142: 'The term "children with specific learning disabilities" means those children who have a disorder in one or more of the basic psychological processes involved in understanding or in using language, spoken or written, which disorder may manifest itself in imperfect ability to listen, think, speak, read, write, spell or do mathematical calculations. Such disorders include such conditions as perceptual handicaps brain injury, minimal brain dysfunction, dyslexia, and developmental aphasia. Such term does not include children who have learning problems which are primarily the result of visual, hearing, or motor handicaps, of mental retardation, or emotional disturbance, or environmental, cultural, or economic disadvantage'.

Students with learning disabilities may:

1. have poor organisation and time management;
2. be slow to start and complete tasks;
3. have a short attention span and difficulty controlling behaviour;
4. have difficulty following oral or written instructions;
5. have an inability to remember what has been taught on a day-to-day basis;
6. have poor social skills due to inconsistent perceptual abilities;
7. show difficulties in fine and gross motor development;
8. show difficulties in orientation to time and space.

In some countries different terms are used to describe learning disabilities (*eg* specific learning disabilities, dyslexia). The following statement in

Dyslexia: A Teaching Handbook offers a clear definition of dyslexia (specific learning disability):

> The Code of Practice, HMSO 1994 in England defines dyslexia as: 'Some children may have significant difficulties in reading, writing, spelling or manipulating number, which are not typical of their general level of performance. They may gain some skills in some subjects quickly and demonstrate a high level of ability orally, yet may encounter sustained difficulty in gaining literacy or numeracy skills. Such children can become severely frustrated and may also have emotional and/or behavioural difficulties.'
>
> (Thompson and Watkins, 1998)

Thompson and Watkins write that there are symptoms of dyslexia which teachers and/or parents can observe which could help in the identifying process. These include:

1. a puzzling gap between written language skills and intelligence;

2. delayed and poor reading and spelling;

3. bizarre spelling;

4. left/right confusion and directional difficulty;

5. sequencing difficulties;

6. poor short-term memory skills (following instructions, repeating digits).

Thompson and Watkins' book contains many remediation techniques and appendices with examples for use in teaching such as phonic work sheets, common words for a basic sight vocabulary word lists, spelling rules. It is an excellent book for a head to read and a must for the Learning Resource Centre library.

It should be emphasised that teachers need instruction in recognising the symptoms of dyslexia which cause students to make errors in mathematics. Chinn and Ashcroft (1998) write that these symptoms are similar to dyslexia in writing and reading and give numerous examples to illustrate how these symptoms can be recognised in mathematics:

1. directional confusion;

2. sequencing problems;

3. visual-perceptual difficulties;

4. spatial awareness;

5. short-term and working memory;

6. long-term memory;

7. speed of working;

8. the language of mathematics;

9. word skills.

Chinn and Ashcroft state that in many cases, children with dyslexia in mathematics need to be instructed as if they were beginning a basic mathematics programme – right from the beginning – to be re-taught the concept of number, early recognition of numbers and their values, the language of mathematics, early number work, the visual sense of number and visual clues to number concepts, number bonds, place value, numbers near to 10, 100 or 1000. The book introduces the student to all the basic facts and continues through the entire basic mathematics curriculum and is also a must for a head to read and a resource for the Learning Resource Centre library.

'A learning disability is often inconsistent. It may seem worse at some times than other and may cause problems in only one specific academic area. Very often when persons are NOT placed in appropriate academic programs, they experience academic failure and poor self-esteem. It is not uncommon for students with learning disabilities to drop out of school or to be passed through the system, never mastering the skills necessary for academic success and post-secondary training for employment'

(New Mexico Learning Disabilities Association, 1998).

It would be beneficial for schools to encourage a close collaboration between the ESL teachers and Learning Support teachers as it is often difficult to distinguish between what is an ESL problem and/or a possible learning disability. Checklists should be created which would provide early warning signs of a possible learning disability with ESL students, especially those just beginning to receive instruction in English. When ESL students can write basic stories, they might be administered *The Test of Written Language* (TOWL-3), PRO-ED publishers. This is an excellent screening test where students write a short story while looking at a picture. Usually, a trained learning support teacher can distinguish between an ESL problem and a learning disability in the written form.

Gifted learning disabled

The National Association for Gifted Children (NAGC) in the United States wrote a position paper on children who are both gifted and learning disabled which could become a policy statement for these children at international schools and is worthy of reprinting here in full. This position paper was included in a handout at the November 1998 ECIS conference at Hamburg by speaker, Dr Carolyn R Cooper PhD in the session 'Integrating Gifted Education into the Total School Curriculum: Practical Tips for Administrators':

'Due to a specific learning disability, an increasing number of students are not achieving up to their potential despite the fact that they demonstrate high ability or gifted behaviour. These students exhibit characteristics of both exceptionalities: giftedness and learning disabilities. Their gifted behaviours often include keen interests, high levels of creativity, superior abilities, abstract thinking, and problem-solving prowess. Similar to their peers with learning disabilities, they frequently display problems in one or more of the following: reading, writing, mathematics, memory, organisation, or sustaining attention. Because of their dual set of seemingly contradictory characteristics, gifted learning disabled students may develop feelings of depression and inadequacy and consequently may demonstrate acting-out behaviours to disguise their feelings of low self-esteem and diminished academic self-efficacy.

'NAGC recognises three types of students who could be identified as gifted learning disabled:

1. Identified gifted students who have subtle learning disabilities;

2. Students with a learning disability but whose gift has not been identified;

3. Unidentified students whose gifts and disabilities may be masked by average school achievement.

'School policies concerning identification and entitlement to specialised educational services can contribute to the under-identification and inappropriate programming for these youngsters. Given that gifted learning disabled students do not necessarily perform below grade level, discrepancy analysis should be based on their potential compared to their classroom performance. Student assessment must include consideration for the time these youths require to complete tasks; the support needed from others to complete each task; and the level at which the student can fairly be predicted to achieve based on measures of potential.

'Identifying students' abilities and gifts should be based neither on classroom performance nor on total test scores in achievement or intelligence. Rather, to identify students' gifts, schools should analyse individual subtest scores and patterns on tests of intelligence as well as emphasise authentic assessment of talent within specific domains using student products, auditions, and interviews.

'Students who have both gifts and learning disabilities require a dually differentiated programme: one that nurtures their gifts and talents while accommodating their learning weaknesses. Being dually classified is often key to students' receiving appropriate services. A comprehensive programme will include: provisions for the identification and the development of talent; a learning environment that values diversity and individual talents in all domains; educational support that develops compensatory strategies including the appropriate use of technology; and school-based counselling to enhance students' ability to cope with their mix of talents and disabilities. Without appropriate identification and services, the gifts of these students will likely be lost.'

(Students with Concomitant Gifts & Learning Disabilities
NAGC, December 1998 p12).

A recent study, *Compensation strategies used by high ability students with learning disabilities who succeed in college* (Reis & McGuire 2000), concluded that gifted learning disabled students often did not receive appropriate education at the high school level and needed to access their university learning centre to be able to continue at the university. 'Many high school students who do not learn compensation strategies in an appropriate elementary or secondary school learning disability and/or gifted program will clearly not learn the skills necessary to succeed in ... post-secondary education.'

It was concluded that 'educators must re-examine the approaches used at the elementary and secondary levels to address the special education needs of students with learning disabilities, including gifted learning disabled students. Pull-out programs that focus on remediation may, in the long run, be detrimental if instruction in compensatory strategies and self-advocacy is not incorporated in an inclusive approach that fosters self-reliance, a critical factor in the arena of higher education'.

Gifted underachiever

"Teachers often agree that one of their biggest frustrations in the classroom is a student who doesn't work up to his/her potential. Kids who can, but won't. The academic underachievement of high ability students is a universal concern among educators, yet we are surprisingly naïve in our efforts to effectively do anything about it. How do we get kids motivated to do what they're capable of doing?" (Maureen Neihart 2003, private conversation). McCoach and Siegle (2003) write that factors that differentiate between high-achieving gifted students and underachieving gifted students were their 'attitudes toward school, attitudes toward teachers, motivation/self-regulation, and goal valuation'. But, these two groups did not differ in their attitude toward their academic self-perceptions. This is an important finding as further research will be needed to substantiate this finding in order to be able to design individual plans to include this factor. Storrs, CT: The National Research Center on the Gifted and Talented, University of Connecticut.

Reis (2000) in her article *The Underachievement of Gifted Students: Multiple Frustrations and Few Solutions,* lists eight elements which interfere with gifted students achieving: 1) non-challenging curriculum, 2) underachievement may be periodic and episodic, 3) parental issues, 4) peers, 5) students not involved in the extracurricular activities and non participation in school activities in general, 6) lack of developing regular patterns of work and homework, 7) lack of a caring adult at the school as a mentor, and 8) inappropriate and unmotivating curriculum. She concludes that too few interventions have been provided to help reverse underachievement and it was to this end that the research on underachieving gifted students was conducted at The National Research Center on the Gifted and Talented. The research is described below.

Although there are underachieving students of all intelligences, the gifted underachiever is one of the most difficult to treat. The National

Research Center on the Gifted and Talented defines a gifted underachiever as a student who:

'shows evidence of potential for high academic performance by meeting at least one of the following criteria:

- Individual IQ test score (either Stanford Binet LM or WISC-III) of at least 120 given no earlier than six years of age OR

- Composite standardised achievement test scores (administered within the past three years) in the 90th percentile AND

The underachiever shows evidence of lower than expected academic performance by meeting both of the following criteria:

- Has grades in the bottom half of his or her class in reading/language arts and/or math OR has a C average or below in reading/language arts and/or math

- Is recommended by classroom teacher, gifted specialist and/or counsellor as being a bright underachiever.'

(National Research Center on Gifted and Talented Children, 2002)

The Center is conducting a study to explore how students might reverse their patterns of underachievement by placing participating students in one of the five goals and treatment groups:

- *Valuing the goals of school*
  Goal – Build task value into the student's academic experiences
  Technique – Classroom strategies and individual meetings.

- *Self regulation*
  Goal – Address time management, goal setting, and record keeping
  Technique – Individual tutorials.

- *Student perceptions of the school environment*
  Goal – Recognition of negative impact of inaccurate perceptions
  Technique – Tutorials emphasising responsibility and choice.

- *Self-efficacy*
  Goal – Increase student's academic confidence in the classroom
  Technique – Classroom strategies.

- *Curriculum compacting and interest-based enrichment*
  Goal – Provide challenging content and work in area of interest
  Technique – Streamline the curriculum.

The study was to be completed in May 2003 with a minimum amount of follow-up data during the 2003-2004 school year. An international school could design IEPs for underachieving students along the guidelines from the study above but it is recommended that the school contact: <rlm02009@uconnvm.uconn.edu> for all information about the study and its results and ask for recommendations in order to put into place the design.

Another source of information about the gifted underachiever can be found on the internet at <http://www.gifted.uconn.edu/reishebe.html> Reis, S M, Hébert, T, Diaz, E I, Maxfield, L R, & Ratley, M R (1995). *Case studies of talented students who achieve and underachieve in an urban high school*. (Research Monograph 95120).

Attention Deficit Hyperactivity Disorder (ADHD)

The criteria for ADHD have been taken from the American Psychiatric Association's Diagnostic and Statistical Manual (DSM-IV) and are broken into three distinct types:

1. Attention Deficit/Hyperactivity Disorder – Predominantly Inattentive, if criterion A (1) is met but not criterion A (2) for the past six months;

2. Attention Deficit/Hyperactivity Disorder – Predominantly Hyperactive-Impulsive, if criterion A (2) is met but not criterion A (1) for the past six months; and

3. Attention Deficit/Hyperactivity Disorder – Combined Type, if both criteria A (1) and (2) are met for the past six months.

Diagnostic criteria

A. Either (1) or (2):

(1) **Inattention:** At least six or more of the following symptoms of inattention have persisted for at least six months to a degree that is maladaptive and inconsistent with developmental level:

(a) often fails to give close attention to details or makes careless mistakes in schoolwork, work, or other activities;

(b) often has difficulty sustaining attention in tasks or play activities;

(c) often does not seem to listen when spoken to directly;

(d) often does not follow through on instructions and fails to finish schoolwork, chores, or duties in the workplace (not due to oppositional behaviour or failure to understand instructions);

(e) often has difficulties organising tasks and activities;

(f) often avoids, dislikes, or is reluctant to engage in tasks that requires sustained mental effort (such as schoolwork or homework);

(g) often loses things necessary for tasks or activities (*eg* toys, school assignments, pencils, books, or tools);

(h) is often easily distracted by extraneous stimuli;

(i) often forgetful in daily activities;

(2) **Hyperactivity-Impulsivity:** At least six of the following symptoms of hyperactivity-impulsivity have persisted for at least six months to a degree that is maladaptive and inconsistent with developmental level:

Hyperactivity

(a) often fidgets with hands or feet or squirms in seat;

(b) often leaves seat in classroom or in other situations in which remaining seated is expected;

(c) often runs about or climbs excessively in situations in which it is inappropriate (in adolescents or adults, may be limited to subjective feelings of restlessness);

(d) often has difficulty playing or engaging in leisure activities quietly;

(e) is often 'on the go' or often acts as if 'driven by a motor';

(f) often talks excessively;

Impulsivity

(g) often blurts out answers before questions have been completed;

(h) often has difficulty awaiting turn;

(i) often interrupts or intrudes on others (*eg* butts into conversations or games)

B. Some hyperactive-impulsive or inattentive symptoms that caused impairment were present before age seven years.

C. Some impairment from the symptoms is present in two or more settings (*eg* at school or work and at home).

D. There must be clear evidence of clinically significant impairment in social, academic, or occupational functioning.

E. The symptoms do not occur exclusively during the course of a Pervasive Developmental Disorder, Schizophrenia, or other Psychotic Disorder and are not better accounted for by another mental disorder (*eg* Mood Disorder, Anxiety Disorder, Dissociative Disorder, or a Personality Disorder.

(Reprinted with permission from the Diagnostic and Statistical Manual of Mental Disorders, 1994, Fourth Edition, Text Revision. Washington, DC, American Psychiatric Association)

ADHD in the classroom

Ochan Kusuma-Powell and William Powell in *Count Me In!* (2001) describe the characteristics of children with possible ADHD in the classroom. These characteristics could be used as a checklist for teachers to determine if a possible referral for the identification of ADHD were to be made:

'Chronic difficulties in maintaining alertness or 'staying tuned' when listening or reading:

- staying focused on the right information for the right amount of time
- filtering out distractions
- poor attention to detail or coping with a series of instructions
- staying on-task

Patterns of procrastination, disorganisation and underachievement:

- activating and organising for work
- choosing the right piece of information on which to concentrate
- accessing short-term memory
- responding accurately to tasks and completing work
- planning and monitoring work and behaviour

Behaviour management issues, such as:

- leaving one's seat without permission
- making noises
- seeming not to listen
- requiring close supervision
- talking out during quiet time'

(Ochan-Powell & Powell, p128-129, 2001)

If teachers observe some of these behaviours another source of information can be found in discussing these behaviours with the student and eliciting his/her concerns. Comfort in Ochan-Powell & Powell (p 129, 2001) describes some of the concerns the student might be experiencing at school:

- worried that they will not be able to follow instructions;
- scared that they cannot finish their work;
- embarrassed about the quality of their work;
- concerned that they are unable to transfer ideas from their minds onto paper;
- frustrated that they are unable to control their behaviours and moods;
- afraid that teachers and peers will be annoyed with them;
- anxious about losing track, day dreaming, checking out and needing to move around.

It is important that the head and staff at an international school be informed about the nature of ADHD and present consistent and uniformed statements about ADHD to questions posed by parents and members of the international school community.

ADHD is a neurobiological disorder, which can be explained as a chemical imbalance in the brain. Often medication is required to manage ADHD. Medication does not change the child but corrects the chemical imbalance in the brain so that the child can maximize learning and deal with daily life. (Medications for ADHD have been researched more frequently than any other group of medications.) However, medication for ADHD by itself is usually insufficient for a child coping with ADHD. Usually some type of behaviour intervention will also be necessary. It is the child's paediatrician in consultation with parents who make the decisions to give medication and not international school personnel.

Some teachers who are uninformed and biased about treatment of ADHD have been observed to try to block the administration of medication to children in their care, if the child needs to take the medication during school hours. This can only cause confusion and more stress for the parents who obviously only want what is best for their child. Parents have often been made to feel guilty about allowing their child to be medicated. A lack of understanding about what ADHD is and how it can be treated results in negative, heated debates among international school personnel. The school head and/or LRC personnel should be well informed about ADHD and train their staff to understand and recognise the symptoms of this disorder. It is recognised that there are cultural differences regarding the use of stimulant medication for ADHD. Handouts on how to work with ADHD children are included in Appendix C, *Handouts*.

In 1998, the Journal of American Medical Association published a Council Report titled *Diagnosis and Treatment of Attention Deficit/Hyperactivity Disorder in Children and Adolescents*. This is one of the most important and comprehensive studies to date. The objective of the study was 'to deal with public and professional concern regarding possible over-prescription of attention-deficit/hyperactivity disorder (ADHD) medications, particularly methylphenidate (Ritalin is in this group), by reviewing issues related to the diagnosis, optimal treatment, and actual care of ADHD patients and of evidence of patient misuse of ADHD medications' (Goldman, Genel, Bezman, Slanetz 1998).

The authors conducted a search of all studies (studies in English only) dealing with children of elementary school through high school from 1975 to 1997. It was concluded that 'Although some children are being diagnosed as having ADHD with insufficient evaluation and in some cases stimulant medication is prescribed when treatment alternatives exist, there is little evidence of widespread over diagnosis or misdiagnosis of ADHD or of widespread over-prescription of methylphenidate by physicians' (Goldman, Genel, Bezman, Slanetz 1998).

It is recommended that schools obtain this article and require their staff to read it and to use it as objective, research-based information for talking with parents. In addition, a useful article from the American Academy of Pediatrics (AAP) giving the standards of identifying ADHD for paediatricians can be downloaded from the Internet: 'Diagnosis and Evaluation of the Child with Attention-Deficit/Hyperactivity Disorder: Practice Guidelines' (*Pediatrics*, Vol. 105, May 2000. URL: <http://www.aap.org/policy/ac0002.html>).

A new medication for ADHD, Atomoxetine, which is not a stimulant medication, is currently being studied extensively by researchers in the United States. Four major studies about Atomoxetine were found on the Internet at the Medline website (6 April 2002):
<http://www.ncbi.nlm.nih.gov/entrez/query.fcgi?CMD=Text&DB=PubMed>

An excellent Internet site for parents of children with learning difficulties is SchwabLearning.org. One of the topics covered by SchwabLearning is *AD/HD, Stimulants, and Substance Abuse* which provides a comprehensive explanation of the subject and is simply written and informative. This site also contained the citation for Atomoxetine, the new medication for ADHD (SchwabLearning, 23 January 2002; and an update in March 2003. <http://schwablearning.org/Articles.asp?r=426>).

The US Federal Drug Administration gave the go-ahead for distributing Atomoxetine in 2002 and it is currently being administered in the United States to children with ADHD.

Emotional and Behavioural Difficulties

It is not easy to define behavioural problems in children, as all children (and actually all adults) may show certain behavioural problems at certain times. The difference for those children with special problems is in the frequency and depth of their problem behaviour and in the situations in which they act up, *ie* the intensity and duration (Gallagher, 1989). The All Handicapped Children Act (US Public Law 94-42) identifies serious emotional disturbance as a category of Special Needs and defines the term in this way:

'... a condition exhibiting one or more of the following characteristics over a long period of time and to a marked degree, which adversely affects educational performance:

1. an inability to learn which cannot be explained by intellectual, sensory or emotional factors;

2. an inability to build or maintain satisfactory interpersonal relationships with peers and teachers;

3. inappropriate behaviour or feelings under normal circumstances;

4. a general pervasive mood of unhappiness or depression;

5. a tendency to develop physical symptoms or fears associated with personal or school problems.'

(Federal Register 1977, p42,478 in Gallagher 1989)

The child showing emotional and behaviour disturbances needs to be observed closely to determine the ways in which they can be helped. The school psychologist should be consulted and if there isn't one on staff, an outside professional should be consulted. A possible referral system might be as follows:

1. Teacher observes child in class and makes notes on behaviours, including the date of the occurrence, noting in particular:

   • duration;

   • prevalence;

   • 'triggers';

   • context;

   • responses (peers).

   The teacher also talks to the child about the behaviours concerned and notes the responses.

2. Teacher consults other teachers who know the child and informs the head.

3. Parents are consulted and asked for input. Other testing may be carried out *eg* formal achievement, intelligence and psychological testing, interviews, behaviour checklists.

4. Case report is written.

5. School psychologist is consulted.

6. Intervention.

7. Regular meetings of all professionals and the parents, to evaluate the programme.

It is essential that all stages of the process are documented as underlying reasons for the emotional or behavioural difficulties may be quite complicated and outside professionals need access to all the facts.

Autistic Spectrum Disorders

Children who are diagnosed with this type of condition may show a range of behaviours, varying from complete withdrawal from the world around them, to being able to function at a very high level in certain areas. 'No one has found a cure for autism, the neurological disorder that leads to lifelong impairments in a child's ability to speak, respond to others, share affection and learn. But there is a growing consensus that intensive early intervention is both effective and essential – the sooner the better' (Tarkan, L. 2002).

An article in *TIME* magazine (July 15th, 2002), stated that the incidence of autistic spectrum disorders seems to be increasing and indeed anecdotal data would confirm this. Certainly, in some schools, the incidence of children showing 'autistic type behaviour', (difficulties with social interaction, social communication and imagination, stereotyped behaviour), seems to be increasing.

Whether schools are able to provide appropriate programmes for the child is very dependent on the school, as some children may require individual tuition or may be able to participate in the class activities with the support of an individual assistant. Children with Asperger's Syndrome, a syndrome related to the higher functioning end of the autistic spectrum, are able to function well in a school situation with the right support and, as adults, are able to contribute to the work force. For further information in this area, consult the web sites: <http://www.autism.com>

<http://www.autismeurope.arc.be>   <http://www.nas.org.uk>
<http://worldautism.org>   <http: www.aspergersyndrome.org>

Culture and language shock

Children arrive in international schools from many different cultures. Suddenly being transferred into another country, another language, another school could have an enormous impact on a child's emotional stability. Some children show symptoms of 'culture shock' whereby they are somewhat traumatised by their new environment. There are many different behaviours, which might be observed (*eg* sullen, withdrawn behaviour, acting up, avoidance of group activities).

Since this is a frequent occurrence at international schools, teachers should be very sensitive to these types of behaviours and allow the child time to adjust to their new environment. By pairing the child with a child who speaks the same language or pairing with an extrovert child, the new child may feel less isolated. Many of our students could be suffering from both language and culture shock. Another major problem is to identify learning difficulties in children who are bilingual/multilingual and who are just learning English.

Useful references for these difficulties in international education are:

- At Home Abroad website includes links to articles and services of interest to expatriates. 27 April 2002. <http://iht.com/athome.html> At Home Abroad welcomes IHT reader comments. Write to: Editor, At Home Abroad, International Herald Tribune, 6 bis, rue des Graviers,

92521 Neuilly-sur-Seine, France. Fax: ++33-1-41-43-93-38, e-mail: athome@iht.com

- Eriksen, M (1999). 'What the global nomads think.' *is-The ECIS Magazine*, 2(1)p33

- Haldimann-Foreman, M (1983). 'Learning Difficulties and the Bilingual/Multilingual International School Student', *International Schools Journal*, 6, Autumn, p59-76

- Haldimann-Foreman, M (1981). 'The Effects of Language Shock and Culture Shock on Students in International Schools', *International Schools Journal*, 2, Autumn,p74-82

- *Language Shock, Dyslexia Across Cultures*. A BBC video and multimedia pack updated regularly on: <http://www.ditt-online.org>

- National Multi Cultural Institute. 24 April 2002. <http://www.nmci.org/>

- Schaetti, B. Transition Dynamics. 24 April 2002. <http://www.transition-dynamics.com/resources.htlm>

- Schaetti, B. Transition Dynamics. 24 April 2002. <http://www.transition-dynamics.com/bibs.htlm>

Child abuse

This is a very sensitive subject that cannot be ignored. Schools should have a policy to deal with suspected cases. Often there are different cultural expectations from parents regarding punishment and although schools should be aware of cultural differences, it is the school's host country along with the school's policy, which determines procedures.

Children suffering from child abuse may show certain behaviours that alert the teacher and imply that something is not right with the child. The child may become withdrawn or defensive or the abuse may be as obvious as the teacher noticing marks on the child's body. There are different cultural expectations for discipline and although schools should be aware of this, it is essential that at all times, children are protected. The school's host country will have certain rules in place and procedures to follow, *eg* in some countries, if the suspected cases are not reported, this may result in prosecution of the individual teacher and the school. Therefore it is recommended that schools formulate a welfare policy that deals with cases of suspected child abuse and that they are in line with the laws of the host country.

Should a teacher suspect that a child has been abused, the principal should be informed immediately and then all meetings and conversations that take place regarding this issue should be documented, together with when and where the suspected abuse was observed and what was seen. Documentation should be factual and unemotional, as this evidence may need to be used in a court of law. Teachers should refer to the procedures in their school policy and remember that even if their suspicions are incorrect, their readiness to listen may already have helped the child tremendously.

Post Traumatic Stress Disorder – helping kids cope with trauma

Since September 11, 2001 schools have become increasingly aware of post-traumatic stress disorder. The following will provide schools with a range of information not only on the disorder but also on school crisis management. 'Information on Post Traumatic Stress Disorder and Crisis Management' was written by Jennifer Henley of *Executive Shortcuts* in the free email newsletter for international educators, *Shortcuts,* October and November 2001. <http://www.international-ed.com/freepublications>

Authors' comments

For additional information about PTSD, Dr Gisela Perren-Klingler (1996), a world expert on PTSD, has edited *TRAUMA: From Individual Helplessness to Group Resources*. The complete coordinates for this book can be found in the Appendix E, *Resources*. An excellent handout for parents, *Trauma And Children: A Parent Handout For Helping Children Heal* by Lazarus in 1996, has been published by the National Association of School Psychologists in the United States. The handout can also be used with teachers for discussions on trauma.

Chapter Three

Policies

Why are we doing this?

"You know, I really wish we didn't have an Open Admissions Policy."

Most international schools provide their clientele with the school's philosophy of education, which includes mission statements, aims and objectives. As part of this section, reference should be made to the Optimal Match model as providing access to the curriculum for all students enrolled in the school. These statements could include respect for individuality, appreciation of student development, and respect for student pace of learning. The school policy manual could include a brief statement about Optimal Match and statements such as:

1. to provide additional individual support and enrichment through a Learning Resource Centre and in the regular classroom;

2. to train teachers by offering in-service workshops as to how to deliver a curriculum to suit the needs of individuals in their care;

3. to provide a wide variety of learning experiences and varied assessments so that students of all abilities are accommodated.

Statements should be written about the procedures used in the assessment, identification, and accommodation of students with specific learning disabilities, exceptionally high academic abilities and talents, and other specific groups that the school will enrol. Ideally, students requiring extra learning support within a Learning Resource Centre should not be charged for this support. As most international schools do not charge students receiving extra support for English language learning, the school's tuition should include the costs of extra learning support. It is the author's opinion that parents of children who require special needs instruction should not be punished financially because their child has specific learning needs.

The following points could be considered while introducing a Special Needs programme to the staff and board members:

- have in place strong unified leadership that invites initiatives into the school setting and supports them with appropriate resources;

- the structure of the school K-12 should reflect flexibility that permits appropriate initiatives for Special Needs students;

- start on a small scale with a specific ability, or set of abilities, that can be advanced with a school's available resources, time, money, personnel. Take into account realistically an institution's strengths and weaknesses. Build on its strengths;

- proceed incrementally. Begin with a small but demonstrable success;

- brief faculty, parents, and students well before initiatives begin;

- advertise initiatives well and place them within the policy and philosophy of the school;

- have initiatives grow out of regular course work with instruction from the classroom teacher;

- define teacher professionalism as imparting knowledge, stretching the imagination, and placing the child in an Optimal Match situation;

- be vigilant against boredom of students and staff resulting from unwarranted repetition of skills and content;

- always balance rigorous and challenging educational course work with a social experience that encourages a realistic assessment of learning, enthusiasm, self-confidence and creativity;

- schools should not bear sole responsibility for the nurturing, both educational and emotional, of children and youth. The imaginative use of other institutions, to include the family, museums, universities, clubs and churches, contributes decisively to meeting the challenge. If a school cannot match a realistic assessment of its instructional strengths and weakness with the development of a student's demonstrated talent, community resources should be sought;

- the artificial lock-step of education (kindergarten through graduate school in discrete units and in predetermined progression) should give way as much as possible to permit students to progress at their own rate in particular areas of study. Students, therefore, could be placed simultaneously at various levels of instruction depending upon the development of academic talent in a particular area;

- educational continuity from class-to-class, grade-to-grade, and level-to-level is the key element in the success of initiatives for highly capable youth;

- appropriate credit, placement or recognition should be given for work which advances or completes the regular curriculum;

- establish a rigorous *descriptive* and *empirical* method of evaluating the success of an initiative on behalf of highly capable children and youth. Be sure that a demonstrable difference has been made educationally as a direct result of intervention. Build the evaluation methodology directly into the initial program design.

> (*Points to Consider When Forwarding Initiatives for Highly Capable Students in American-Sponsored Overseas Schools*, Durden, 1988)

The following two policies, one for learning difficulties and one for the gifted and talented, are examples of how different international schools address the special educational needs of their students.

1. Foundation of the International School of Geneva (Second Draft – 1996)

Learning Support philosophy

Learning Support is concerned with students:

- The school recognises that students have different learning styles and it will provide appropriate teaching, within its resources.

- Some students have specific learning problems. It is the responsibility of the school to recognise and diagnose these needs, and provide an appropriate educational plan for these students.

- There may be some students whose immediate academic and/or social needs are clearly beyond the provision of the Foundation. In such cases the student will not be admitted, or only allowed to continue under very clearly defined conditions which will be subject to regular review.

- A number of students in our school will have temporary or more long-term learning needs which require support additional to the normal classroom teaching. The school will provide professional advice and, within the limit of its resources, appropriate help. Some students with learning difficulties may have access to local resources but this does not reduce the school's responsibility towards them.

Learning Support is concerned with teachers:

- All teachers have a role to play in supporting students who have special learning needs. They will be assisted by the Learning Support specialist teachers and the school psychologists.

- The school recognises that a teacher's understanding of learning differences and language developmental needs leads to more imaginative and effective learning for the whole class. The school's staff development plan must take this into account.

Learning Support is concerned with parents:

- Parents are seen as partners and will be expected to cooperate with the school in assuming joint responsibility for addressing the student's learning needs. They will be consulted, kept informed and actively encouraged to support their child's learning.

- At the time of admission parents should provide any relevant information which will help the school organise the most appropriate programme for the student.

- Parents are responsible for ensuring that their child regularly attends school and makes full use of the educational support programme that has been arranged by the school and mutually agreed to by the parents.

Learning Support is concerned with programmes:

- It is the school's aim to integrate all students into the mainstream classes where they will receive appropriate teaching and support.

- Teaching styles should reflect the wide range of abilities and language levels present in most of our classes, even at the most advanced level.

- The majority of students in the higher grades will pursue academic courses leading to university or college education. The Senior Secondary School will also offer programmes or options which lead to a recognised certificate/diploma (*eg* IB certificates, Graduation Diploma *etc*) which will allow students to progress to an appropriate post secondary experience.

- It is the school's responsibility to give advice where and when appropriate, if it is evident that either local or other alternative programmes/schools appear to be the better option for the student.

Learning Support is concerned with resources:

- The Foundation accepts responsibility for providing appropriate services for the students it enrols, within the guidelines laid down for 'students' and 'programmes' in this document.

- The Foundation recognises that Learning Support specialist staff is the most important resource it can provide in this area.

- There will be occasions when the school will recommend to parents the possibility of specialist tuition over and above what the school can provide.

Learning Support policy for primary schools

Learning Policy:

- The curriculum, teaching methods, resources and expectations of the primary school will be suited to the wide range of potential, levels of attainment and different learning styles represented by the student body.

- The responsibility for the Learning Needs of the primary school child rests with the classroom teacher supported by the principal, assistant principal, Learning Support teachers, the school psychological services and the parents.

- Learning Support in the primary school will be in the form of assistance and support to the classroom teachers and will be integrated into the normal classroom programme. It is acknowledged that at times, however, support outside the classroom is in the best interests of the student.

Admission/screening:

- All primary school students will be screened on entry. A further screening process will be carried out in class four.

- A child with a severe learning disability may be admitted to the primary school with the clear written understanding of the nature and time span of the school's commitment.

- If, after admission, the principal finds that the child's educational needs are beyond what the school can offer, s/he reserves the right to ask the parents to choose an alternative school provision. This applies, in particular, to the admission of the very young child.

Diagnosis/testing:

- The class teacher's personal observation of the child's performance is the first method of identification of Learning Needs. This is reinforced by consultation with parents and previous teachers. No method of identification will be used in isolation and, following referral, appropriate diagnostic tests will be carried out.

- Following testing, children requiring Learning Support will have an educational plan prepared for them by the classroom teacher and the Learning Support teacher. After approval by the principal, this plan will be shared with parents.

- The student's progress will be monitored and their programme reviewed and evaluated regularly. The principal and parents will be kept informed at least once per term.

Provision:

- Each primary school in the Foundation will have, proportionate to enrolment, the same minimum number of teaching periods allocated to Learning Support. This will provide mainstream support and/or small group support to children diagnosed as having Learning Needs.

- Individual tutorials billed to parents may be arranged in exceptional cases when the child's Learning Needs are greater than can be met by normal school provision. In all cases these children will have (or have had) help provided by the school. The parents will give their prior written agreement.

- The curriculum development plan for each school will take into account the need for all the members of the school teaching staff to be kept up to date with the best of current theory and practice in the field of Learning Needs.

Learning Support policy for middle and secondary schools

Learning policy:

- The curriculum, teaching methods, resources and expectations of the middle school and secondary schools will take into account the wide range of capability, prior learning and different learning styles represented by the student body.

- The responsibility for the learning needs of the middle school and secondary school child rests with all of the child's teachers, supported by the principal, assistant principal, Learning Support teachers, the guidance counsellor, the school psychological services and the parents.

- Learning Needs in the middle school and secondary schools will be in the form of assistance and support for the subject teachers, and this could be reinforced with group tutorials under the guidance of a specialist Learning Needs teacher. It is acknowledged that at times individual support sessions may be in the best interests of the student.

Admission/screening:

- The former school of every new student will be required to submit details of any Learning Needs support that it has been necessary to provide, including all appropriate testing results that are available. This information will be provided directly between the former school and The International School of Geneva.

- All middle school and secondary school students will be screened on entry. The results of this screening will be discussed with the Learning Support specialist before final placement is decided. Further tests will be given if this appears appropriate, and in consultation with the parents if it appears possible that a student may be experiencing learning difficulties.

- A child with a severe learning difficulty may be admitted to the middle school or secondary school with a clear written understanding of the nature and time span of the school's commitment.

- If, after admission, the principal finds that the child's educational needs are beyond what the school can offer, s/he reserves the right to ask, and aid where possible, the parents to choose an alternative school provision.

Identification procedures:

- A subject teacher's personal observation of the child's performance may be the first method of identification of Learning Needs. This is followed up by consultation with the Learning Needs specialist who will contact the child's other teachers. If it is determined that Learning Needs support is required, the parents will be advised in writing and appropriate testing will be carried out. Parents and students themselves may seek the advice of the Learning Needs specialist.

- Following testing, a child requiring Learning Needs support will have an Individual Educational Plan (IEP) prepared by the Learning Needs Department, in consultation with the guidance counsellor (where appropriate), the Educational Psychologist, and the child's teachers. The principal will be informed of the IEP, and this plan will be shared with the parents.

- The progress of these students will be assessed, their programme reviewed and evaluated regularly, and the results will be discussed with the student and parents.

Provision:

- Each middle school and secondary school in the Foundation will have, proportionate to enrolment, the same minimum number of periods allocated to Learning Needs. This will provide mainstream support and/or tutorial support for children identified as having Learning Needs.

- Individual tutorials billed to parents may be arranged in exceptional cases when the child's Learning Needs are greater than can be met by general school provision. In such cases the parents will give their prior written agreement.

- The professional staff development plan for each school will take into account the need for all members of the school teaching staff to be kept up to date with the best of current theory and practice in the field of Learning Needs.

- Parents of children with identified Learning Needs will be advised of and provided with a full description of all of the educational options provided by the school, available within the local community, and in alternative schools.

(Reproduced with kind permission of The Foundation of International School of Geneva, June 2, 2002)

Authors' comments

The above policy is currently in revision.

2. Providing for the highly capable at an International School

Overview

What is reflected, above all, in the mission, aims and objectives at many international schools is a determination to respect the needs of the individual student and a commitment to match those individual needs with an appropriate learning environment. In a diverse cultural population at international schools, this commitment continues to be a tremendous challenge. Each academic year receives students of mixed language ability coming from a wide variety of school systems from around the world. Many of these students have Special Needs beyond the most obvious need for English language instruction.

The highly capable student – a definition

Students with special academic talents (including the arts) joining our school may or may not have been identified before entry. It is valuable for us as a staff to be aware of key behaviours of the highly capable student so that we can best serve the child. Renzulli's (1978) Schoolwide Enrichment three-ring concept of giftedness is a valuable starting point to help shape our approach to these student's specific needs. According to Renzulli, a student who is 'gifted' demonstrates above-average ability in one or more domains, and displays creativity and has a commitment to task. Another way to define the highly-capable student is through considering the student's *Precocity, Intensity and Need for Complexity* (Javits Institute, Skidmore, NY 1995).

What we don't often see in any student population, and particularly at an international school, is the 'perfect all-rounder', a top student who excels in every discipline and demonstrates the need for broad-based acceleration. More often, we have students with talents in specific disciplines or domains. To honour those talents, and challenge our highly capable child, we must have at hand a range of options, if we are to have success in meeting his or her needs. The first and crucial step is identification.

Identifying the highly capable student

Identifying the highly capable child or youth takes the form of a procedure, similar to identification of the child with learning difficulties. We should strive for an accurate assessment, employing a variety of means to measure the talents and identify the needs of a student. Indeed, a palette of information packages and screening tools is required to get a full picture of the student, including, most importantly, the following:

- Teacher observations.

- Intelligence tests.

- Performance measures (not just grades, but other activities, hobbies, prizes won, portfolios, that will provide possible evidence of talent).

- Checklists such as the Cummings checklist and interest inventories.

- Aptitude and Achievement Tests – this may include (for aptitude) the Ross Test of Cognitive Abilities, the Cornell tests, the PSATs, the SATs and PLUS test, and (achievement/aptitude) the ERB CTP III Achievement and Ability tests, for example. A test of a child's non-verbal reasoning skills may also be appropriate, for example, the Raven Progressive Matrices. Out-of-level testing, to determine the student's 'ceiling' could, for example, involve giving end-of-year placement exams to certain students at the beginning of the year.

- As a resource, the CTY International Talent Search programme (for 12 to 13 year-old students).

In terms of general screening for the highly capable student, the efforts on the part of teachers and the Learning Support team would include casting 'as wide a net as possible' to discover talent, (*Educational Resources for Academically Talented Adolescents,* CTY Publications and Resources, The Johns Hopkins University, 1994, p.25). There is no one predictor of academic talent, but a range of tools should be used to indicate a student's particular area of strength. We also need to be 'good detectives' to uncover and establish the depth and degree of a specific talent. Curriculum compacting would be one logical accommodation for students who need acceleration in a specific area.

A recommended procedure

Similar to the referral process for students with suspected learning difficulties, the procedure to identify the depth and degree of a student's specific talents will follow several steps. The task of defining a set of specific criteria for determining whether this child or that child is a candidate for any enrichment programme remains open, a worthy topic for discussion in the near future. With that question still open, the following procedure is a starting point for the Learning Support Unit and the teaching staff:

1. A referral form is filled out by a classroom teacher, accompanied by information taken from the student's previous school in his/her file in the main office, samples of classroom work, test results, project samples, grade reports, standardised test results. Or, a referral form is filled out by the Educational Psychologist after classroom observations and a collection of work-samples is gathered including information taken from the student's previous school in his/her file in the main office. The Cummings checklist would also be very useful at this stage. A request for permission for testing would be sent out to the child's parents.

2. At the same time, the parents might already be involved if they have provided information about the child's particular talents or interests. In some cases, a parent has already had the child tested and will provide a written report. These reports are useful; they will not replace, however, the procedure that our own LSS unit and the Educational Psychologist will carry out.

3. Initial screening utilizing a range of aptitude tests, including the DTLA-3, and achievement tests in specific subjects, such as mathematics, science, language arts. Group achievement test results from the ERBs, for example, are brought in to enhance the student portrait.

    a. In-depth testing, usually with the Wechsler tests takes place to identify the child's intellectual talents and strengths.

    b. Conduct an inventory of the child's interests.

    c. Issue a written report including results and recommendations, which will be discussed with the child's teachers and sent to the student's parents where appropriate.

    d. Avenues of differentiation can be discussed by concerned teachers and LSS staff. At this point an IEP is devised with accommodations or programme plan. Depending on the family situation, parents can be brought in for an open discussion about the outcomes for their child.

    e. On-going assessment and evaluation of the effectiveness of the devised programme is essential to assure that we are on target with meeting the child's needs.

Accommodations

We need to have available a wide range of options, remain flexible and look to using as many community resources as possible when designing a programme for a highly capable child. Among many accommodations, we must consider the following:

- enrichment in a specific area – within or outside of the classroom;
- 'pull-out' enrichment programmes (small groups, when appropriate);
- curriculum compacting;
- CTY Distance Learning and all related talent-search procedures, including SAT testing for possible summer school experience in the USA or other countries (*eg* CTYIreland, Germany);
- advancement to the next grade or in a specific subject;
- contests, competitions;
- independent projects – not just busy-work in the library, but a process that could very well involve a mentor (community-based, when possible/ appropriate).

Conclusion

Our success in meeting the needs of the highly capable child at international schools will perhaps be best reflected when classroom teachers speak with relief (!) and confidence that 'no stone has been left unturned' in finding ways to accommodate his or her very bright children. At the same time, it is highly recommended that our teaching staff review and consider the needs and behaviours of highly capable children in the form of, perhaps, a series of in-service workshops. This kind of training would be on-going, ideally, and explore good teaching practices for the full range of student learning styles and needs in the regular classroom.

(Deborah Ott, International School of Berne, September 2001. Reproduced with kind permission from the author.)

Authors' comments

Please see a description of the CTY International Talent Search and Compacting in Chapter 6, *Programme delivery and accountability*. Another example of school policy can be found on the internet: <http://www.nc.uknet> from the British National Curriculum. There is a page devoted to 'developing an institution-wide policy' for the gifted and talented and covers:

- policy rationale and aims;
- definitions;
- identification;
- provision;
- organisational issues;
- transfer and transition;
- resources;
- monitoring and evaluation.

More sites can be found on the internet by conducting a Google search using 'learning disabilities and policies', for example.

Enrolment criteria

Children coming from different international schools have different backgrounds, different educational experiences and different educational needs. The difficulty in establishing enrolment criteria is: what is the mission of the school? Is it to provide education to all students who apply to the school? Or is it to provide the best possible education that fulfils all their educational needs? The school's Special Needs policy and criteria for admitting children should be very clearly articulated both to parents and teachers. The policy should outline the steps to be taken if children were admitted and found to have learning needs that the school can or cannot accommodate. Similarly, as a student's learning needs change, the school must be very honest with the parents and continually re-assess the provision. If the school cannot meet the needs of the students, the school should give adequate notice for the parents to start looking for a more appropriate placement. The bottom line is honesty. State what services can be provided and furnish the parents with an accurate assessment of their child's needs.

The parents have the responsibility to furnish the school with as much information as possible about their child's learning. Therefore, the school should request detailed information on the admissions form about student learning needs. Due to the transient nature of the international school population, records and test results may not always be readily available. They may have been conveniently 'forgotten' or unintentionally misplaced or 'arriving in the next shipment'!

This is why the parents should be required to complete a detailed admissions form (a copy of which should be placed in the student's file), outlining their child's learning needs and giving as much information as possible to the school (*eg* pertinent medical conditions including vision and hearing, referrals for testing and test results, a section where the parents can provide additional information useful in providing an optimal match for the school to the child). The admissions office should inform members of staff about any new student arriving during the school year so that none in need of learning support fall through the net. Obviously special learning needs may only emerge later, and the school should be prepared to deal with these issues.

To begin the identification and assessment process it is recommended that a qualified staff member, familiar with the assessment and identification of Special Needs students, read every student file for any 'red flags'. Important information for the student can then be quickly transferred to a Student Cumulative File Checklist (a sample can be found on page 69). This document summarises the most important and relevant information required by all teachers and should be circulated to all appropriate staff members. However, it is still important for classroom teachers to read the files of all their students carefully as the more information a teacher has about a student, the better his/her learning needs can be met.

Chapter Four

Organisation, services and personnel
Who does what?

"OK you guys – get yourself organised ... those who can, this side, those who can't but have a permit, this side, all those who don't mind having a go, this side. The rest of you, over that side."

Procedures

In order to present the argument for the development of a Learning Resource Centre (LRC), the areas of organisation, services, and personnel have to be addressed. These areas should be carefully planned and include details on the following:

- budgeting;
- type of services offered;
- job descriptions;
- hiring procedures;
- staff development;
- creating student study teams;
- programme descriptions and instructional aims;
- space;

- facilities;
- equipment;
- resource materials.

All of these areas should be included in an LRC policy and curricula guide, which should be updated frequently as a means of evaluating the LRC functions. It is also recommended that the school brochure include a description of the LRC. Creating study teams to analyse student needs is essential rather than assigning just one person the responsibility for identifying students in need of specialised services. The International School of Barcelona has developed an extensive study team model, which reflects the Optimal Match concept and has proven very effective (Haldimann,1998). Parents are very sensitive to the idea that their child may have special educational needs, and a study team approach gives the parents more confidence in the school's approach to Special Educational Needs than the possible 'subjective' opinions of just one teacher.

Tahmincioglu (2001) wrote an article in the *International Herald Tribune* to emphasise the importance of hiring qualified personnel whether for the LRC or as regular classroom teachers. He quoted David Dunning, a professor of psychology at Cornell University in New York: 'It's very difficult for incompetent people to know they are incompetent.' '…Most incompetent people actually tended to think more highly of themselves than their competent colleagues. It is a workplace Catch-22: If you think you are incompetent, you probably are not, but if you think you can do no wrong, you almost certainly can and will. When people are incompetent in the strategies they adopt to achieve success and satisfaction, they suffer a dual burden. Not only do they reach erroneous conclusions and make unfortunate choices, but their incompetence robs them of the ability to realise it' (Tahmincioglu, 2001).

The authors have lived through the pains of working with unqualified LRC staff and the lack of LRC teacher evaluation processes in international schools. The bottom line is the provision of a quality programme for students. It should be regular policy to offer a new teacher a trial period within the LRC rather than a one- to three-year contract. It is strongly emphasised that the learning support staff reflect a healthy personality and the ability to communicate with different groups of the international community. The head needs to consider carefully all aspects of the interview process and have a set list of procedures for hiring LRC teachers as well as for regular classroom teachers.

To help school heads in recruiting Special Needs personnel, a list of hiring tips and questions to pose during interviews are included later in this chapter. The organisation of service and personnel should be on-going with frequent evaluation of staff. Also included are sample job descriptions for a Learning Resource Centre coordinator, Learning Resource Centre teacher, classroom support teacher and for an Educational Psychologist. It is extremely helpful to have an Educational Psychologist on site to be able to assess students with in-depth tests only available to Educational Psychologists or psychiatrists, and to run the LRC. Ideally, if the Educational Psychologist were also able to give counselling in addition to testing, that would eliminate the need for another staff position.

Organisation

It is recommended that schools draw up a flow-chart to clearly show the structure of the Learning Resource Centre. Multiple copies should be available to anyone who inquires about the organisation of the LRC. The chart should be placed in the LRC policy and curriculum document as well as in the school's policy manual.

Services

It is very important for a Learning Resource Centre to present its services in written form in its policy and curricula guide, the general school policy manual and as copies to give to anyone who inquires about the services.

The Support Services Department

An example of how one school advertised its learning support services

The Support Services Department provides academic support and English as a Second Language to students of all levels, and communicates with and offers advice to teachers and parents. The department offers support in:

English as a Second Language (ESL)	Grade K-12
Language Arts support (reading, spelling, comprehension, writing)	Grade 1-8
General curriculum support	Grade 9-12
Study skills	Grade 1-12
Speech therapy	Nursery-12
Physiotherapy	Nursery-12
Occupational therapy	Nursery-12
Individual tuition	Nursery-12
Psychological services	Nursery-12
Academic testing	Nursery-12

The Support Services Department meets once per week to discuss student concerns and general business and the teachers join grade level meetings and faculty meetings when these occur.

(Mandy Macleod, Director of Support Services, St John's International School, Belgium, August 1994).

Personnel

It is essential for schools to invest in the hiring of well-qualified, experienced LRC staff. The job descriptions included here describe the basic minimum requirements for employment in the LRC at an international school.

Job descriptions

The following job descriptions should be considered basic for an effective Special Needs/Learning Support programme. These descriptions may seem idealistic compared to what is currently in place at your school, but it should be stressed that without the right people a school will not have a truly effective programme. The LRC personnel need to be strong in their convictions and be able to remain firm when confronted by angry, threatened and worried parents and teachers, and have the ability to stay 'cool' under difficult situations. They also need to demonstrate a healthy personality and not be in the profession because they 'need to be needed'.

Job description for a Learning Resource Centre teacher

The Learning Resource Centre teacher will be responsible for teaching students within the LRC who have learning difficulties/differences and/or students who have been identified as having academic talents and gifts. This will be with supervision from the Educational Psychologist and/or within the regular classroom with supervision from the regular classroom teacher.

A. Qualifications for this position include:

1. Masters Degree in Special Education or other specialist qualification and evidence of recent professional development if degree is more than seven years old.

2. At least three years teaching in an international special education environment.

3. Demonstrable knowledge in the areas of Learning Disabilities, ADHD, Gifted and Talented, Emotional and Behaviour Problems, Computer Instruction, Educational and Psychological Testing.

4. Demonstrable knowledge of screening tests, how to administer these tests and how to write a screening report.

5. Demonstrable ability to write IEPs and to carry them out.

6. Knowledge of host country language or willingness to learn the language.

7. The personality and the ability to communicate effectively with different groups of people (*eg* students, parents, school staff, director, school board, PTA, outside agencies).

8. Willingness to attend Optimal Match Network Institute and to incorporate Optimal Match practices in the work environment, if Optimal Match is integrated in the school.

B. Policy and curriculum:

1. Consults and adheres to the LRC Policy and Curriculum Guide.

2. Participates in end-of-year evaluation of LRC policy, curriculum and LRC itself.

3. Conducts teaching as prescribed in the LRC Curriculum Guide.

4. Develops IEPs for all student in his/her charge with supervision from the school's Educational Psychologist or LRC co-ordinator with input from classroom teachers, parents, and students, where appropriate.

5. Writes daily lesson plans from the IEPs and maintains files of student work to show evidence of effectiveness of the IEPs and lesson plans.

6. Arranges scheduling of students in his/her charge.

7. Maintains a supply of blank forms for referrals, checklists, *etc* for use in LRC and for teachers.

C. Conferencing:

1. Confers with Educational Psychologist and/or LRC co-ordinator with original referrals to the LRC, student entrance and exit to the LRC with consultation from significant persons regarding the learning needs of the LRC students.

2. Confers with Educational Psychologist and/or LRC co-ordinator about suggested changes in LRC student instruction.

3. Guides staff with the referral process, if necessary.

4. Administers screening tests (highlighted on screening form by Educational Psychologist or LRC co-ordinator) to students referred for screening, relates the screening results as soon as possible orally and in written form, and participates in the decision making for in-depth testing with LRC team.

5. Is responsible for presenting screening results during conferences with staff, parents and students, where appropriate.

6. Participates in the second half of conferences with parents after the in-depth testing results have been reported to the parents by the Educational Psychologist.

7. Receives supervision for completed IEP forms and confers with appropriate classroom teachers about the subject matter to be covered in the LRC and/or regular classroom. If there is to be only classroom help, the teacher, LRC teacher and the Educational Psychologist will participate in the writing of the IEP for classroom support.

8. Informs significant faculty members of projects, mentorships and research topics with which the LRC students will be working.

9. Maintains membership in a professional organisation related to Special Educational Needs.

Job description for classroom support teacher

The classroom support teacher probably will be one of the LRC learning support teachers who will also give special lessons within the LRC along with supporting regular teachers within the classroom. Therefore, the qualifications section for the learning support teacher would apply to the classroom support teacher.

Responsibilities:

1. The classroom support teacher (CST) will give small group instruction within the general classroom environment under the supervision of the classroom teacher and the LRC co-ordinator. The position of the CST does not include asking teachers if they need classroom support, rather, the classroom teachers will request classroom support by completing a request form indicating who will be instructed, for how many periods per week and type of support requested. The form will be discussed between the LRC co-ordinator and the future CST and permission granted.

2. Upon approval of classroom support, the CST will meet with the classroom teacher, and together they will complete a Classroom Educational Plan (CEP) for each student. The plan would include specific areas of instruction, time and day of support, present level of performance, semester objectives, resources, criteria for achievement, and semester evaluation of each student. The Classroom Educational Plan will be kept in a folder within the classroom which will help classroom teachers plan instruction and provide parents with information about their child's instruction. The folder should also contain group lesson or individual lesson plans and a type of diary form for each student's participation in the lesson.

3. Students with specific learning disabilities may be included in group work but not worked with alone in the classroom environment. If individual lessons were required for students with specific learning disabilities, LRC teachers will provide instruction within the LRC. This also applies to students who require individual enrichment for high academic abilities and talents. The CST's responsibility to provide support or reinforcement of the class instruction, which the classroom teacher provides and the CST should not be asked from the classroom teacher to teach specific reading or math groups. Those are the job of the classroom teacher.

4. The CST should make a general schedule of classroom support including the number of periods and specific classrooms where the support will be given by the end of the first week each semester. The schedule and each Classroom Educational Plan should be copied and given to the LRC Co-ordinator.

5. At the end of each semester, the CST and regular classroom teacher should evaluate the classroom support and the Classroom Education Plan for each student and complete instructional objectives for the following semester. At the end of each school year the 'plans' should again be evaluated by the CST and teacher and recommendations made on the 'plan' for the next school year.

6. Other activities that the CST may be invited to participate in could involve the teacher's initial screening of all students, the organisation of ERB test books, answer sheets, and directions for classroom administration. The CST may also be asked to act as a reader by the LRC or classroom teachers for students taking the ERB tests.

Job description for Learning Resource Centre coordinator

The Learning Resource Centre coordinator will assume administrative duties in addition to his/her responsibilities to the Learning Resource Centre (LRC). This is a paid position on top of the individual's regular salary within the LRC. The Learning Resource Centre co-ordinator will be part of the school's team approach to providing services from the LRC to the school. It may be that the Educational Psychologist in addition to his/her responsibilities could fill the LRC co-ordinator position. This would be an ideal situation, but an experienced learning support teacher may also qualify for this position.

A. Qualifications for this position include:

(these qualifications are about the same as some of the LRC support teacher and Educational Psychologist, but we have seen people put in charge of an LRC who have only counsellor training and know nothing about running an LRC and nothing about standardised testing, learning disabilities, IEPs, gifted and talented students. Thus a job description for the LRC co-ordinator is essential.)

1. Masters Degree in Special Education or in a related field.

2. At least three years experience in the field of Special Education, two of which within the school's LRC, if possible.

3. Demonstrated knowledge in the areas of Learning Disabilities, Gifted and Talented, Computer Instruction, Educational and Psychological Testing.

4. Ability to speak host country language, if possible.

5. Demonstrated healthy personality and the ability to communicate effectively with different groups of people (*eg* students, parents, school staff, school board, PTA, outside agencies).

6. Willingness to attend Optimal Match Network Institute and to incorporate Optimal Match practices in the work environment, if Optimal Match is practised at the school.

B. Responsibilities:

1. Policy and curriculum:

   a. Oversees utilization of LRC Policy and Curriculum Guide.

   b. Enforces standards which stay within the confines of the 'spirit of the law' in host country, United States, and United Kingdom.

   c. Supervises Individual Educational Plans (IEP, CEP) development for students.

   d. Supervises written statements on students seen by LRC staff providing support within regular classrooms.

   e. Responsible for revising policy, curriculum and procedures, designing or redesigning forms, when necessary.

   f. Encourages LRC teachers in providing word processing, spell checking and keyboarding skill-building for students attending the LRC.

   g. Conducts end-of-year evaluation of services writing goals for following school year, supervises student transfer documents from LRC.

2. Conferencing:

  a. Conducts regular meetings (informal and formal) with LRC staff.

  b. Meets with director at least once a week to discuss LRC concerns.

  c. Acts as representative/spokesperson at staff and PTA meetings, and outside agencies, when necessary.

  d. Acts as guide and consultant to visitors to LRC.

  e. Provides avenues for LRC staff development and all school staff development regarding issues pertaining to Special Needs students.

  f. Makes recommendations for staff attendance at the Optimal Match Network Institute, if the school practises Optimal Match.

  g. Arranges in-service workshops for all staff about LRC issues.

  h. Maintains membership in a professional organisation related to Special Educational Needs.

3. Clerical:

  a. Provides faculty with list of current LRC students and students receiving LRC help within the regular classrooms.

  b. Sends letters requesting permission to parents to sign for student participation in the LRC programme.

  c. Provides written reports requested from schools regarding former LRC student participation.

  d. Maintains LRC space on staff bulletin board.

  e. Provides staff with articles pertinent to the LRC issues.

  f. Remains cognizant of current LRC income and expenditures.

  g. Orders materials for LRC, when necessary.

Job description for an Educational Psychologist

The Educational Psychologist will be part of the team approach to the school's Special Needs/Learning Support programme. This person will be available for consultations within the LRC, with staff, students and their parents. It would be ideal if the Educational Psychologist were also trained to counsel students as the student should be seen globally for his/her educational and psychological needs.

A. Qualifications for this position include:

  1. A Masters Degree in psychology or school psychology.

  2. Experience working within an international school environment, if possible.

  3. Speaks host country language or is willing to learn the language.

  4. Has knowledge and experience in administering group standardised tests.

  5. Follows the medical model in writing evaluation reports.

6. Demonstrates knowledge of students with varying Special Educational Needs.

7. Shows ability to communicate to various groups within the international school community.

8. Willingness to attend Optimal Match Network Institute and to incorporate Optimal Match practices in the work environment, if the school practises Optimal Match.

B. Policy and curriculum:

1. Consults and adheres to the LRC Policy and Curriculum Guide.

2. Attends end-of-year evaluation meeting on LRC policies, curriculum and LRC itself.

3. Supervises the Learning Resource teachers and provides guidance in writing IEPs, CEPs and lesson plans.

C. Identification of Learning Disorders and/or exceptional gifts and talents:

1. General Information Gathering:

   a. Reads student files with emphasis upon:

      i. detecting discrepancies in school reports;

      ii. comparing test results and discrepancies;

      iii. participation in Special Education and/or Gifted programmes;

      iv. medical issues.

   b. Examines the school's ERB group standardised test results and K-2 screening results for student discrepancies and high scores within and between yearly testing programmes and 'red flag' any student showing discrepancies to LRC co-ordinator.

   c. Follows up on discrepancies/high scores by consulting appropriate school staff, parents, students and outside agencies and requests further information from former schools and parents.

   d. Requests observation of targeted students, referral forms and checklists for screening and/or in-depth testing from teachers and parents.

   e. Provides training in identification and treatment of students with special needs, including how to read screening and in-depth testing reports.

   f. Provides training for LRC teachers for utilising various screening tests and how to write a screening report.

D. Assessment:

1. Requests parental permission by staff for student screening and in-depth testing.

2. Supervises screening and administers in-depth testing, when necessary.

3. Supervises screening follow-ups and administers in-depth testing follow-ups.

4. Supervises screening reports, writes in-depth testing reports and consults with all significant persons regarding test results.

5. Meets regularly with director and LRC staff.

6. Contacts outside agencies regarding student special needs (*eg* psychiatric evaluations, resources for exceptionally gifted and talented students).

E. Coordination and administration of testing (*eg* K-2 screening and ERB testing or similar):

1. Supervises screening of K-2 grade students:

   a. Responsible for test preparation, administration, supervision and correction of screening tests.

   b. Responsible for reporting student discrepancies and/or high capabilities to teachers and recommendations for student learning support.

2. Supervises standardised tests Grades 3-10 with Educational Records Bureau Comprehensive Testing Program (ERB) IV or similar tests:

   a. Responsible for ordering, preparation of instructions, designing and conducting test preparation for students, staff and parents.

   b. Responsible for proof-reading and sending answer sheets/books to testing agency for machine scoring, hand-scoring some tests, when necessary.

   c. Responsible for test result statistical analysis including training the school staff in how to use test results.

   d. Responsible for providing test comparisons over time to staff and parents.

F. Professional development:

1. If the school uses the Optimal Match programme the EP will strive to meet Optimal Match assessment requirements; conducts Optimal Match training session in his/her field of knowledge.

2. Attends conferences relating to special needs/learning support.

3. Reads monthly LRC journals and provides articles for staff as appropriate, and maintains LRC resource library (books, journals, articles, software, curriculum guide).

4. Maintains membership of a professional organisation related to special educational needs.

All Educational Psychologists do not have the same training, and one must be careful in hiring an EP as the school personnel, parents, students and people within the community tend not to question the competency of an Educational Psychologist. Here is an illustration, a true story, of what can go wrong when the Educational Psychologist is incompetent:

'My daughter was referred for testing as she was having difficulties with writing. The school psychologist decided to administer the WISC-III test of intelligence. After receiving the written report, the results showed that my daughter had serious problems in verbal processing. This seemed rather strange to me as my daughter is extremely gregarious, had never had any difficulties in this area and was obtaining good grades where verbal processing was essential. However, despite being a Special Needs teacher, I did not think to question the somewhat bizarre results as a school psychologist is considered a professional. It was only after asking for a copy of the test results, that I began to be concerned. I asked for an independent analysis of the results by another school psychologist. It was only then that I realised that my daughter's results had not only been scored incorrectly but false conclusions had been drawn from the incorrect results. This caused my daughter to feel that she was a failure and she was branded as being a failure by the teachers and lost a lot of self-confidence. By the way, my daughter never received testing for writing difficulties, the referral question'

(a concerned mother, 2002).

Some suggested questions to ask candidates for the position of Educational Psychologist:

1. What is your experience with group standardised testing of ability and achievement of students? And what is your opinion of group standard-ised testing in general at international schools?

2. How many Wechsler scales have you administered? Which scales? And could you provide a sample educational achievement testing report from your diagnoses and recommendations of students with Learning Disabilities, ADHD, Gifted/Talented or a combination of these Special Needs for students in your charge? Please include a Wechsler student profile with all the scaled scores included.

3. What is your opinion about giving out the Wechsler information to parents and school staff members?

4. What is your opinion of medication for the treatment of ADHD?

5. What are the topics of workshops or in-service you have presented and where have you presented?

6. What type of parent involvement do you think is necessary with students receiving learning support?

7. What are your favourite resources for learning support for different stu-dents you will be testing and making recommendations?

8. What are some of the problems you have encountered as an Educational Psychologist, and how have you dealt with them?

9. What experience do you have in diagnosing learning disabilities, gifted/talented, ADHD with ESL students? Could you describe the difference between typical ESL errors and dyslexic errors in writing tasks?

10. What do you know about dyslexia and mathematics?

11. What are some of your favourite computer programs for students receiving learning support?

12. What is an IEP and could you send a sample of an IEP you have written along with the sample testing report?

13. Will you please also send a list of the tests that you administer as an Educational Psychologist?

14. Do you have experience with providing counselling to students and parents, and if so, could you please describe typical cases you have worked with?

15. What do you know of the Optimal Match concept?

Hiring Learning Resource Centre (LRC) personnel

For many years, the teacher training materials at the Center for Talented Youth (CTY), Baltimore, Maryland, have contained a list of the characteristics of successful teachers of highly gifted children. Essentially, this is just good teaching for all teachers. A partial list of these characteristics was published in the 2000 CTY annual report as:

- Knows the subject – handles it with confidence, and inspires students to love the subject.

- Knows excellence and can demand it – sets high standards for work and personally lives up to them.

- Learns from and listens to students – see students as full participants in the class, learning from them and assuming that they will be able to provide new insights into the subject.

- Possesses a sense of humour – demonstrates that knowledge and its exploration can be engaging, lively, and fun.

- Likes both teaching and young people – enjoys students and the interplay of the classroom.

- Builds communities – regards the class as a community and creates an atmosphere where students can be curious and explore knowledge in a supportive place.

- Says "I don't know" when he or she does not know the answer.

- Is interesting and interested – is open to a world of ideas beyond the confines of the subject at hand.

- Possesses mental flexibility – stretches beyond the narrow confines of the subject and tolerates ambiguity as the class explores the meaning and substance of the discipline.

- Pursues personal and professional growth – views the students and their responses in class as a stimulus for growth.

- Uses many teaching methods – adapts to students and draws upon a variety of teaching strategies to convey the subject.

(Center for Talented Youth 2000)

These characteristics of good teaching apply to all teachers in an international school including LRC personnel. Also included are Dr Carolyn Cooper's effective teachers list, personal quality list and hiring tips (ECIS Conference Handout, Hamburg 1998). These examples also apply to LRC personnel and the regular classroom teachers at an international school:

Effective teachers of bright, talented students:

- have been successful teachers in the regular classroom;
- are experts in at least one content area or on one topic;
- know and apply principles of talent development;
- differentiate curriculum and instruction according to individual students' strengths;
- distinguish coaching from coaxing;
- are confident in their own abilities;
- neither fear nor resent bright students;
- encourage students to chase their dreams;
- know how much to expect and when to demand it;
- hold firmly to standards of high quality;
- with the student: evaluate student products according to criteria used by professionals;
- in the specific fields of endeavour students have pursued;
- distinguish positive feedback from empty praise;
- 'go to bat' for kids who want to make a difference.

Personal qualities:

- a sense of humour;
- resourcefulness;
- open-mindedness;
- flexibility;
- good communication;
- productivity;
- creativity;
- willingness to acquire additional training in gifted education.

Tips for hiring your talent development specialist

On a scale of 1 to 10:

- What does this teacher believe bright, talented individuals should do in this world?
- How effective is this teacher in the regular classroom?

- To what degree is this person a 'natural' teacher?
- How much and what type(s) of experience has this teacher had in teaching bright, talented students?
- How compatible with our district's (school's) philosophy about bright students and intended student outcomes is this individual?
- To what degree does this individual believe in the power of students to make a genuine difference in their world?
- How committed is this teacher to creative production? What evidence do I have that he/she is a creative producer?
- How sophisticated are products this teacher's students have produced?
- How current is this person in gifted education pedagogy?
- How effectively does this teacher implement the Principles of Differentiated Curriculum with students?
- How willing is this teacher to acquire further training in gifted education as needed?
- How does this candidate rate when compared with the effectiveness of my best teacher of bright, talented students?
- How much training will this teacher need to be successful with bright, talented students in our district (school)?
- What does this teacher believe was his/her most important achievement as a youngster? As an adult to date?
- What does this teacher want me to know about him/her and why?

(Cooper 1998)

Chapter Five

Assessment and identification
Who gets what?

"So, what label does he deserve today?"

It is essential that international schools develop assessment and identification policies, which are adhered to by all staff and are consistent with the school's mission, aims and objectives statements.

1. Role of testing

Educational screening and testing are an essential component of the Optimal Match Concept. It is strongly recommended that there be a uniform and consistent procedure to identify type and degrees of specific learning disabilities, academic abilities and talents of highly capable students, some of whom may also have specific learning disabilities, ADHD and/or emotional problems. ESL students in all stages of English language learning and students with gaps in their education due to frequent changes of schools and languages need to be assessed for accurate placement and instruction. Good teaching follows accurate diagnosis. Assessment information is also important for student transfer to home country or to other international schools. Due to differences in the grading process between schools, student test results from a standardised test may be the only objective information to be received from the former school.

Norm reference and criterion reference tests are considered helpful since they provide reference points in determining the best fit between students and educational expectations. An excellent article *Standardised Tests: Still an Essential Option for International Schools* (Mills and Durden, 1996) has been included in Appendix C, *Handouts* to help clarify the issues of standardised testing in international schools. This article, which is research based, may be useful when formulating testing policies.

Teacher-made tests or in-house assessment instruments are also considered appropriate to complement norm and criterion reference tests as well as student portfolios. (Purcell and Renzulli, 2001, have written an excellent portfolio aid: *Total Talent Portfolio: A Systematic Plan to Identify and Nurture Gifts and Talents.* Please see Appendix E, *Resources.*) The use of *multiple* measures of assessment is important for comprehensive, reliable, and valid assessment as well as for confirmation of assessed abilities and knowledge. This also implies that a team approach to the assessment and identification of students with special educational needs should be in place before the process commences.

Assessment objectives

Appropriately selected and administered assessment instruments by *qualified* and *trained* staff members provide information, which is used for the following objectives:

- to make meaningful placement decisions;
- to document student growth through pre-and post-testing;
- to assist teachers in making more efficient and effective decisions about instructional content and placing of individual students;
- to provide an *objective* measure of student basic skills and reasoning abilities;
- to help identify gaps in basic skills, especially for students who have made frequent changes of schools, instruction, and languages;
- to help identify students with specific learning disabilities;
- to help identify students with exceptionally high academic abilities and talents.

It should be emphasised that the assessment process is a team approach to identify specific learning needs and information gathered from all individuals involved with the child. Indeed, as stated in the Wechsler Intelligence Scale for Children, 'As in all evaluations, assessment information from multiple sources is essential' (Wechsler, 1991, p9).

2. Educational screening and testing phases

The authors emphasise that the educational screening progress is the very first step in the identification process, and regular classroom teachers or resource teachers should not use the screening checklists and screening tests to make the definitive diagnosis. The assessment and identification process is multi-disciplined, and requires information from many sources in order to make the correct identification.

In order to achieve the assessment objectives, educational screening and testing have been divided into four phases plus a fifth phase for evaluation of the complete assessment and identification process:

Phase I – Screening of all students for placement by classroom teachers with the help of learning support staff. The screening would include appropriate placement tests in reading, written expression, and mathematics. The students' scores would be placed on a *Student Progress Sheet* (see example, page 71) to help document student progress over time. Post screening at the end of the school year would enable teachers for the following class to place students more easily at the beginning of the new school year.

The progress sheets should be designed to follow the student from grade to grade. Classroom teachers, in consultation with the learning support staff, should target students who show exceptionally high or low academic scores in any of the student placement test areas for further screening. Lists of appropriate screening test should be provided to classroom teachers, and they should receive training from the learning support staff on how to administer these tests. If classroom teachers are included in the beginning placement and screening processes, they will feel more empowered as student support team members. If the school is fortunate enough to have a large learning support staff, release time could be given to help the teacher administer the screening tests. Some international school heads have given learning support staff the first month of each school year for classroom support to help classroom teachers with placement and screening while giving learning support lessons only to returning students and/or high risk students.

Phase II – It is highly recommended that a group-administered standardised testing programme be developed to measure student achievement and abilities objectively over time. This should be administered relatively soon in the autumn/fall term. If students are tested in the spring, the students' classroom teacher will not have enough time to re-teach or enrich students based on the results of the tests. Testing in the autumn also provides more evidence for the further investigation of students with possible learning disabilities and/ or students with exceptional academic talent. It is inevitable that a number of students will leave after the autumn term or in the middle of the school year, and that there will also be students entering the school after the autumn testing had been completed.

Some group standardised test companies provide hand-scoring templates for students who missed the autumn testing and could be tested upon entrance to the school. In 1985, after extensively researching several group standardised testing programmes, the ECIS Guidance Committee recommended the Educational Records Bureau (ERB) *Comprehensive Testing Program* as a suitable programme for use in international schools (see complete coordinates in Appendix E, *Resources* section).

It is recommended that ESL students whose level of English is adequate to take the test be included in a group standardised testing programme. This includes ESL students with specific learning disabilities taking a non-standard form, if necessary. ESL student test results would serve as a baseline of English language learning and emerging achievements and abilities over time. To help decide which ESL students have adequate English knowledge to be included in a group standardised testing programme, a language rating scale could be could be used to determine the level of English language learning (Haldimann, 1999). The language scale could be one of the ways for determining which ESL students were ready to take a group standardised ability and achievement test.

Many secondary international schools are now administering the *Secondary Level English Proficiency Test* (ETS 1997 see Appendix E, *Resources*) to students in grades 7-11. This test places students into five different categories of proficiency of English and could be used to decide which secondary school ESL students would have adequate English skills in order to take a group standardised test or part of the test.

In addition, a non-verbal test, the CTY Spatial Test Battery (STB), has been developed which could be administered to ESL students in the early stages of English language and subsequently along with maths subtests from a group standardised achievement test until the ESL student is able to be administered the full testing programme (Haldimann, 1999). Results from a study with the CTY STB conducted on sixth grade students at nine international schools world-wide showed: 1) high correlations with potential academic success as measured by grade point average for ESL students as well as native English speakers; 2) when the sample was divided into ESL and native English speakers, the STB did not distinguish between these two groups, indicating that ESL students are not penalised on this test; 3) the study concluded that 'the STB can contribute to reducing the bias against ESL students that is likely to occur when measures of verbal reasoning ability are administered to members of this population' (Stumpf & Haldimann, 1997).

Currently the CTY STB is being administered at Sylvan Learning Centers in the United States as a supplement to taking the SAT reasoning tests for qualification to the CTY Talent Search programme. If the student's SAT Math reasoning score is just below the qualifying point, but the student has high scores on the STB, the student might be qualified for the CTY Talent Search programme. Please see Appendix E, *Resources* for the Talent Search information or go onto the CTY website listed in the *Resources*.

Some international schools also administer the *Test of Written Language-3* (TOWL-3, ProEd Publications), Spontaneous Writing Subtests, to students from the 3rd to 11th grades along with administering group standardised achievement and ability tests. This gives valuable and objective information to teachers about the writing skills of the students and offers immediate placement for the school's writing programme.

Phase III – A formal student referral should be given to the learning support department after the student support team has received and discussed the information from Phases I and II. A sample Student Referral Form can be found on page 78. Students would be referred to the learning resource centre for individual screening. Although this can be done without an educational psychologist it is important that the screening be conducted by a *qualified* and *trained* Special Needs teacher. This person should be able to write a screening report, which can be reported orally to the student study team, with recommendations for accommodations and/or in-depth testing to formally diagnose learning disabilities and/or exceptional abilities and talents.

It is recommended that if an ESL student were referred for screening, if that student's knowledge of English is limited that the appropriate questionnaires and checklists be administered in the student's native language. Usually, someone can be found who speaks the student's language and can make an oral translation of the forms to the student's parents or someone trusted to keep the information confidential.

Screening is a key stage for the school's learning support programme. However, these phases are flexible. A student might be found during the first day/week of school who presents obvious signs and the learning support staff will be alerted. Sometimes, schools will find enough information from the student's file and from the parents for the students to be sent immediately for learning support and/or for an Individual Education Plan (IEP) to be written for the regular classroom. Some students arrive at their new school with an IEP already written from their previous school.

Phase IV – If schools are fortunate to have an on-site Educational Psychologist to administer the in-depth testing, including the Wechsler Intelligence tests, they are in an excellent position to implement the elements of the Optimal Match model. If an Educational Psychologist is not available on-site, it is vitally important to develop a list of external agencies to which students can be referred for in-depth testing. If there is no help available at this key stage, schools will still have a lot of screening and standardised testing information to be able to develop an IEP for a Special Needs student. A sample IEP form can be found on page 83.

A Wechsler Intelligence Profile form (page 80) can aid in understanding the individual subtests and scores from the Wechsler Intelligence Scales. These are essential for the definitive diagnoses of learning disabilities and/or exceptional intellectual abilities. It is highly recommended that the school or parents request all the Wechsler subtests to be administered and the Wechsler scores be recorded in a written report. One global IQ score is not sufficient information in order to include a student's intellectual strengths and/or weaknesses in the IEP. For example, the Wechsler

Intelligence Scale for Children III generates sixteen scores all of which are important to know in order to see a child's intellectual profile.

It is important to obtain permission for screening and testing from the student's parents and inform the parents at each phase. Some student support teams hold conferences with the parents at key stages. It is recommended that a learning support teacher and the Educational Psychologist hold the final conference with the parents and provide the parents with a copy of the IEP developed for their child. Some international schools require the student to help write his/her IEP and for the IEP to be signed by the student and his/her parents. It must be remembered that assessment is an on-going procedure and that IEPs may need to be changed over time.

An international school, which did not have an on-site Educational Psychologist, requested in-depth testing of one of its students from a psychologist with a good command of English in the community. She assured the school that she could administer the Wechsler Intelligence Scale-III (WISC-III) to the student. When the psychologist informed the parents that they should come for an interview after the testing, the results were given orally in the form of a single, global IQ score. The parents reported this to the LRC Coordinator who asked the parents to obtain more information about the 15 other scores which were generated by the WISC-III testing. The LRC Coordinator gave the parents a Wechsler profile form (page 80) for the psychologist to complete. When the parents went to see the psychologist and asked her to complete the profile, she said, "I cannot fill out this form as the scores are a medical secret".

Phase V – Evaluation of each phase should be ongoing and formally evaluated at the end of each school year. Accountability is achieved through successful execution and evaluation of IEPs and requesting the entire staff to evaluate the special learning needs programme either at the end of each term and/or at the end of each school year. Some learning resource centres send out student progress forms regularly to the appropriate staff and hold frequent student case study conferences. Although the staff are busy, it is important to hear the varying comments from different teachers regarding the student. The head's involvement in the evaluation phases is also vital in giving the entire staff the impression that the learning support programme is valuable and supported from the top. It is recommended that the learning support centre's staff develop a workshop about the learning support programme at the school and invite the school's staff, parents and school board members to attend the workshop.

Procedures and forms

One of the first steps in the assessment and identification process is to look at what is already recorded in the student's school file. This is usually stored in a locked cabinet within the school's administrative office. Below is an example of a 'student cumulative file checklist' used to obtain relevant information about the student's past school performance.

Student cumulative file checklist

Please tick and comment where discrepancies exist.
Teacher's Name: Date:
Student's Name: Grade: Birth Date:

❐ **Registration/application form** front page – received Special Education instruction and/or educational testing. Comment:
Back page – medical problem(s). Comment:

❐ **Report cards** (attention/concentration problems, superior or inferior grades, Special Education programme, gifted/talented programme). Comment:

❐ **Standardised testing** (2 stanine differences between scores, percentile rank differences). Comment:

❐ **Reports** (psy/ed testing, Special Education, gifted programme). Comment:

❐ **Correspondence** (former school recommendations, parents/teachers). Comment:

❐ **Other** (please specify). Comment:

Please send a copy of this completed checklist to the LRC if you think further investigation should take place

The referral procedures page below was used at an international school to formalise the process. This avoids the situation where a teacher waylays the Learning Resource teacher in the playground/faculty lounge and discusses concerns about a student who may have Special Needs. Sometimes teachers are loathe to commit such concerns to paper. Communication between staff and LRC personnel should not be denied, but during the conversation the teacher should be asked to make an appointment with the appropriate person to start the referral process.

Learning Resource Centre

Referral procedures

1. Teacher with concerns sees section coordinator:

   a. Teacher should show examples of classwork or describe student behaviour, in the case of a special ability, an example of that ability.

2. Section coordinator arranges conference (including LRC coordinator) with all staff involved with the particular student:

   a. Coordinator takes minutes of conference.

   b. Suggested modifications and intervention strategies should be discussed and tried *before* a referral to the LRC is made.

   c. If a change in student behaviour or performance is not noted after implementation, a referral form should be completed with work samples, when appropriate, and minutes of conference should be attached to the referral form.

   d. Coordinator obtains parental permission for screening and eventual in-depth testing (list response under Additional Comments on referral form which should be handed in person to the LRC coordinator).

3. LRC staff observe student in class (if necessary):

   a. Observations should be noted on back of the referral form.

4. LRC staff arrange screening times and begin screening:

   a. Important results will be relayed orally as screening proceeds.

   b. Note: Screening and testing is a time-consuming process – from two to eight or more periods for screening, at least four or more periods on in-depth testing depending upon the nature of the student's difficulties/abilities.

5. Screening and test results:

   a. Results will be written (see *Assessment report*, page 81) and expressed to staff, parents, and students (when appropriate) in conferences with recommendations for intervention.

6. Learning support:

   a. After testing, if admitted to the LRC, the LRC teachers will either begin intervention within the LRC rooms, enter the regular classroom to help the student or a combination of both.

   b. IEPs (Individual Educational Plans) will be written for each student with classroom and LRC strategies listed, and kept in the LRC room and a copy given to classroom teacher and parents (who will sign the IEP that they agree with the interventions).

   c. Section coordinators will also receive a copy of the IEP for each student to be used in staff conferences regarding the particular student.

   d. Follow-ups will continue on a regular basis in form of parent-teacher conferences, section conferences, mid-term and end of term grades and evaluations from IEPs.

Authors' comments

In the following pages there is a range of forms and checklists to aid the identification process.

PROGRESS SHEET   Name   Date of Birth

	Grade_	Grade_	Grade_	Grade_
Physical (allergies/medical) Social Emotional				
Reading/Phonics Entry Leave				
Spelling Entry Leave				
Maths/Non Verbal Reasoning Entry Leave				
General Comments				

Entry is the first testing at the start of the school year. **Leave** is the second testing at the end of the school year. For example a school may test the students for reading and maths at the start and end of the school year, the results would be placed on the Progress Sheet to be handed on to the teacher of the next grade in the following year.

The sheet can be copied on two sides to cover eight grades if the student stays that long in the school.

Smith classroom behaviour checklist

The following checklists have been reproduced with kind permission of Sally Smith. They can help teachers look for their students' strengths and weaknesses. If a person has a preponderance of ticks in the last two columns, he or she may be demonstrating a number of attentional, organisational, and social immaturity problems similar to learning-disabled students, and needs to be referred for testing. (This checklist can be used as the first step in identifying high potential if there is a preponderance of ticks in the 'usually' column.)

Classroom Behaviour	Usually	Sometimes	Seldom	Never
Extraordinarily observant				
Listens well to instruction				
Follows oral directions well				
Speaks to the point				
Well focused on tasks				
Completes tasks within time frame				
Is on time to classes				
Homework handed in on time				
Follows written directions well				
Tests well, particularly multiple choice				
Good use of space on a page				
Moves well (not clumsy)				
Knows left from right side				
Good handwriting				
Takes good notes				
Neat desk				
Brings necessary materials to class				
Follows procedures carefully				
Good follow-through on projects				
Consistent in responses to questions				
Remembers information well				
Good with symbols and codes				
Good with foreign language				
Good with algebra and chemistry				
Good at organising work				
Alphabetises well, uses library well				
Self-starter				
Adjusts well to changes in routine				
Moves easily from one activity to another				
Can do several things at once				
Welcomes new approaches				
Eager for new information				
Sensitive and considerate of others				
Takes turns easily				

(Copyright 1996 Sally L Smith – reproduced with kind permission from Sally Smith)

Additional Information

When the referral form and the completed classroom behaviour form have been returned to the Learning Resource Centre, the LRC staff should discuss the case and choose checklists to give to the teacher(s) to obtain further information. The LRC staff should also request a conference with the referral person(s) in order to obtain further information.

Smith checklist of characteristics of learning disabilities

Student Name: Date: Birth Date:
Nationality: Language(s):   Grade:
School: Person Completing Checklist:

❐ Do I hate to read?

❐ Do I get headaches when I read?

❐ Do I lose my place when I read?

❐ Do I read very slowly?

❐ Do I mix up *p* and *d* or *b* and *q* or *on* for *no*?

❐ Do I read *8* for *3* or *5* for *2*?

❐ Do I read *llamas* for *small* or *unclear* for *nuclear*?

❐ Do I hate to read out loud?

❐ Do I omit word endings when I read aloud, reading *row* for *rowing*?

❐ Do I have trouble following spoken instructions?

❐ Do I mix up my left side and my right?

❐ Do I get lost easily?

❐ Do I often wish people would repeat what they said?

❐ Do I have trouble comprehending what is said on telephone?

❐ Do I hate talking on the telephone?

❐ Do I often miss the point of jokes?

❐ Do I get confused by puns, plays on words, sarcasm?

❐ Do I have trouble remembering names?

❐ Do I have trouble remembering dates, telephone numbers, and zip codes?

❐ Do I have trouble organising my thoughts?

❐ Do I forget what I was going to say?

❐ Do I forget words I know well?

❐ Do I tend to stutter?

❐ Do I avoid discussions?

❐ Am I a very visual person rather than a word person?

❐ Am I easily sidetracked?

❐ Do I have trouble sitting still?

❏ Am I restless, always moving my feet, my fingers, or my mouth?

❏ Do I have trouble waiting for things?

❏ Am I usually late to work or school?

❏ Do I have trouble reading a watch?

❏ Do I have trouble meeting deadlines?

❏ Do I skip or omit words, sentences, or paragraphs?

❏ Do I have to reread material to understand it?

❏ Do I avoid writing whenever possible?

❏ Do I use the telephone rather than write?

❏ Do I spell badly?

❏ Do I have trouble even writing a thank-you note?

❏ Am I unable to take notes?

❏ Am I unable to fill out forms?

❏ Does my writing look like chicken scratches? Is it tiny and cramped?

❏ Do I hate using scissors, pasting, or tying knots?

❏ Do I have trouble fixing things with my hands?

❏ Do I have great trouble with math?

❏ Are decimals and fractions very difficult for me?

❏ Is long division really difficult for me?

❏ Do I have problems counting change?

❏ Do I have trouble keeping my bankbook straight?

❏ Am I disorganised?

❏ Are my things always in a mess?

❏ Do I lose everything?

❏ Am I over-organised?

❏ Do I have to have everything in place?

❏ Do I have trouble organising myself to begin things?

❏ Do I have trouble paying attention?

❏ Am I very distractible?

❏ Do I have trouble staying on task?

❏ Do I forget to bring necessary things to class or work?

❏ Do I hand my work in late?

❏ Do I have to do one thing at a time to be successful?

❏ Do I have trouble doing several things at once?

❏ Am I inflexible?

❏ Do I hate surprises or changes in routine?

❏ Am I easily overwhelmed?

❏ Do I have trouble breaking things down into manageable chunks so I can begin with one thing, move on the next and then on to the next to finish?

❏ Do I have trouble setting priorities?

❏ Do I avoid making decisions?

❏ Do I start things and never finish them?

❏ Do I tend to back out of things, quit, or not show up?

❏ Am I easily frustrated?

❏ Do I tend to explode when frustrated?

❏ Do people tell me that I'm hard on myself?

❏ Do I exhaust myself from working so hard?

❏ Do I plunge into things without thinking them through?

❏ Do I concentrate on details and miss the main point?

❏ Do I tend to be inconsistent and erratic?

(Smith, Sally (1992) *Succeeding Against the Odds.* p15-18, reproduced with kind permission from the author).

If the student is old enough to complete the Smith checklist, it is recommended that he/she be allowed to complete it answering either orally to a LRC staff member or in written form. This checklist can be brought out to discuss with the student at the recommendations conference and when writing an IEP. Students are usually honest when answering the different questions and by discussing the checklist with a student, he/she feels included in the diagnoses and recommendations for support.

The Smith Checklist contains questions related to symptoms of ADHD. It is suggested that if most of the questions for ADHD are ticked, then the LRC should begin an investigation as to whether the student might have ADHD. There are good parent/teacher/child checklists for ADHD on the market (*eg* Jordan Executive Function Index for Children, Miller Questionnaire for ADHD, Conners' Rating Scales), which should be purchased for the LRC and completed with all pertinent information for a referral to the student's paediatrician.

Cummings checklist©

Characteristics of Gifted and Talented Students

The following list of characteristics, while by no means all inclusive, represents traits found in gifted and creative children. If any student in your class is described by a number of the items on this list, you may want to watch him/her more carefully for possible inclusion in the gifted programme. Those items which are most applicable should be ticked twice. Any supporting information and comments should be written on the back of this form.

❐ 1.   Is an avid reader.

❐ 2.   Has received an award in science, art, literature.

❐ 3.   Has avid interest in science or literature.

❐ 4.   Very alert, rapid answers.

❐ 5.   Is outstanding in math.

❐ 6.   Has a wide range of interests.

❐ 7.   Is very secure emotionally.

❐ 8.   Is venturesome, anxious to do new things.

❐ 9   Tends to dominate peers or situations.

❐ 10. Readily makes money on various projects or activities – is an entrepreneur.

❐ 11. Individualistic – likes to work by him/herself.

❐ 12. Is sensitive to feelings of others – or to situations.

❐ 13. Has confidence in self.

❐ 14. Needs little outside control – disciplines self.

❐ 15. Adept at visual art expression.

❐ 16. Resourceful – can solve problems by ingenious methods.

❐ 17. Creative in thoughts, new ideas, seeing associations, innovations, *etc.*

❐ 18. Body or facial gestures very expressive.

❐ 19. Impatient – quick to anger or anxious to complete a task.

❐ 20. Great desire to excel even to the point of cheating.

❐ 21. Colourful verbal expressions.

❐ 22. Tells or writes very imaginative stories.

☐ 23. Frequently interrupts others when they are talking.

☐ 24. Frank in appraisal of adults.

☐ 25. Has mature sense of humour (puns, associations, *etc.*)

☐ 26. Is inquisitive.

☐ 27. Takes a close look at things.

☐ 28. Is eager to tell others about discoveries.

☐ 29. Can show relationships among apparently unrelated ideas.

☐ 30. Shows excitement in voice about discoveries.

☐ 31. Has tendency to lose awareness of time.

(W B Cummings, 1973. San Francisco Unified School District.
In: ETS Tests in microfiche collection 8788).

Authors' comments

It is recognised that a student with high potential may only be performing well in just a few of the areas from the checklist. It is important to investigate further any ticks placed on the checklist. For example, the student may be highly academically talented in mathematics and may not show many characteristics from a checklist such as the Cummings. It is important that a multi-disciplined team approach be applied to the identification of students with high academic/talented potential.

Student referral for assessment

Referral person: Referral date:

Student's name: Birth date:

Grade: Age:

Nationality: Language(s):

Reason for referral

Interventions tried before referral

Background information (attach work samples where appropriate)

Additional comments

(Please also complete student classroom behaviour form)

Learning Support Centre

Screening checklist for learning difficulties and/or high potential

(The highlighted screening tests are to be administered for this student.)

Student's name: Birth date: Age: Grade: Date:

Criteria   **Assessment instruments**

Academic achievement

Math	Reading	Language
KeyMath	Woodcock Reading	TOWL
Brigance	gates	TOWS
Wdck/Jn	Wdck/Jn	Wdck/Jn
WRAT	WRAT	WRAT
France	Brigance	TEWL
	GORT	Essnt. Eng
	New Read Analysis	PPVT

Cognitive ability

Raven Progressive Matrices (C, S, A)
TONI
Columbia Mental Ability
Ross Test
Urban Tests of Creativity
(Wechsler Scales – administered by
Educational Psychologist)

Information processing

Visual	Auditory	Motor
Slingerland	Slingerland	Slingerland
Detroit Tests	Detroit Tests	Detroit Tests
Aston Index	Aston Index	Aston Index
Beery VMI	Wepman	Beery VMI

Use other side for screening behaviour and observations

Please attach standardised testing results and any other information, which might help in identifying learning difficulties and/or high abilities and talents.

Name: Date: Age: Tester:

Wechsler Intelligence scale for children-III

Test result profile:
Verbal scale
Performance scale
Full scale

Verbal Tests	Below average 1 2 3 4 5 6 7	Average 8 9 10 11 12	Above average 13 14 15 16 17 18 19	Abilities Measured
Information				General ability and motivation to collect knowledge
Similarities				Logical and abstract reasoning ability
Arithmetic				Concentration, attention and numerical reasoning
Vocabulary				Word knowledge and expressive language
Comprehension				Practical knowledge and social judgments
Digit Span				Immediate auditory memory, attention/concentration

Performance tests				
Picture Completion				Visual alertness, long-term visual memory
Picture Arrangement				Ability to plan, anticipate, interpret social situations
Block Design				Non-verbal abstract reasoning, visual perception
Object Assembly				Practical reasoning, visual motor perception
Coding				Eye-hand coordination and speed of new learning
Mazes				Ability to plan ahead, visual/motor coordination
Symbol Search				Visual perception and speed of scanning

3 – 4 point difference in subtest scaled scores is necessary to assume a significant difference
9 – 12 point difference between Verbal and Performance IQ is necessary to assume a significant difference

Verbal Comprehension Index: Perceptual Organisation Index: Freedom from Distraction Index: Visual Processing Speed Index:

Assessment Report Form

Student's Name   Birth Date

Sex   Test Age

Nationality   Language(s)

Grade   Test Date (s)

School   Test Place

Reason for Referral

Tests Administered

Test Behaviour and Observations

Test Results and Analyses

Test Interpretation and Recommendations

Name and Position   Date

Student learning style profile (example)

Student's Name: Pieter   Birth Date: 10 December 1992

Sex: Male   Grade: 4

Nationality: Swiss/German   Language(s): German, English

Assessment Date: 7 Feb 00   Assessment report: Yes, see LRC Ed
Psych

Areas of strength

- high intellectual capacity
- voracious, superior reader
- excellent verbal & nonverbal reasoning
- language learning talent
- high creative ability – likes to invent things
- many interests (*eg* mountain ranges, science, technology, computer, music, drama, magic)

Areas of concern

- relationship with peers
- relationship with adults
- atttention to task
- attention span
- social behaviour

Suggestions for learning

- Offer challenging learning tasks in which he must do research, invent or create a product and present to class.

- Make sure that he has challenging and enriching tasks – try compacting to buy time.

- Give clear expectations with agreement for completion of tasks, and a written contract for longer projects.

- Mix groups carefully so that he must cooperate and contribute meaningfully – find someone who has a 'like mind' to work together on tasks.

- Encourage him to become 'the class expert' on a subject where his peers could seek him out when they had questions on the subject.

- Try the 'Concentration Cockpit' with the whole class and meet with him individually for understanding his class behaviour.

- Model clear messages regarding his social behaviour ("When you say that, you make me feel…"), and explore new ways for him to work out conflicts with peers and adults.

- Reward him for on-task behaviour (*eg* verbal praise, letter home to parents, stickers).

- Try creating a contract with him with a list of positive items for rewards for desired behaviour.

Individual Educational Plan

Student's name:

Birthdate:

Age:

Date of plan:

School:

Grade:

Resource teacher's name:

Annual objectives:

Specific areas for enrichment (E) and/or remediation (R):

| Semester__: School objectives | Resources | Achievement criteria | Date achieved |

| Semester__: Home objectives | Resources | Achievement criteria | Date achieved |

Evaluation and recommendations:

Talent development checklist

Student: Grade: Date: Age:

Evaluation of programme and student progress dates:
Name of evaluator:

Options   tick off

(Please specify areas of talent development on other side of paper for each tick)

Flexible pacing   ❏

Flexible or cluster grouping   ❏

Differentiated instruction   ❏

Curriculum compacting   ❏

Advanced placement   ❏

Concurrent elementary programme with subject   ❏

Acceleration to higher grade   ❏

Concurrent secondary programme with subject   ❏

Acceleration to university placement   ❏

Credit for out-of-school programme   ❏

Independent study   ❏

Distance learning   ❏

Tutorials   ❏

Mentoring   ❏

After-school programme   ❏

Other_____   ❏

Comments: (please use other side, if necessary)

Optimal match modifications and supports checklist

(American School of Barcelona, Elsa Lamb, Former Director)

Student............................ Grade........... Date....................

Modifications needed for this student to assure participation in regular and supportive programmes are specified below. Please tick as appropriate.

Pacing

❐ Extended time requirements

❐ Use written plans/timelines for accelerated or enrichment study

❐ Allow breaks

❐ Vary activity often

❐ Omit assignments requiring copying in timed situations

❐ Provide home set of texts/materials for preview and review

❐ Send school texts home for summer preview

❐ Other..

Environment

❐ Planned seating

❐ Alter physical room arrangement

❐ Define areas concretely

❐ Reduce/minimise distractions

❐ Involve learner in researching/creating interest centres

❐ Other..

Presentation of subject matter

❐ Teach to student's learning style;
     ❐ Visual   ❐ Auditory   ❐ Multi

❐ Individual/small group instruction

❐ Utilise specialised curriculum

❐ Acceleration in .... within regular classroom

❐ Joining another class ....higher grade................
          lower grade..............in ....

❐ Tape lectures/discussions

❐ Provide notes

❏ Functional application of academic skill

❏ Present demonstrations

❏ Utilise manipulatives

❏ Emphasise critical information

❏ Pre-teach vocabulary

❏ Make/use vocabulary file

❏ Make own spelling mistake/correct work dictionary

❏ Reduce language level or reading level of assignment

❏ Use total communication

❏ Share activities

❏ Use visual sequences

❏ Use compacting techniques

❏ Teach keyboarding
    ❏ word processing   ❏ spell check   ❏ grammar & punctuation

❏ Use process logs to document process involved throughout study

❏ Exempt from basis skills work in areas where high level performance demonstrated

❏ Other...

Materials

❏ Arrangement of material on page

❏ Taped texts and/or other classroom materials

❏ Highlighted texts & study guides

❏ Use supplementary materials

❏ Use advanced materials

❏ Note-taking assistance: Photocopies of another student's notes

❏ Typed teacher material/lesson plans

❏ Large printing

❏ Special equipment (calculator, computer, video recorder, *etc.*)

❏ Other...

Assignments

❏ Give directions in small, distinct steps (written, verbal, picture)

❏ Use written backup for oral directions

❏ Lower difficulty level

❏ Shorten assignments

❏ Reduce paper & pencil tasks

❏ Read/tape record directions

❏ Give extra cues/prompting

❏ Allow student to record/tape assignments

❏ Allow student to complete assignments on computer and hand in print-outs

❏ Adapt worksheets/packets

❏ Utilise compensatory procedures by providing alternate assignment/strategy when demands of class conflict with student capabilities

❏ Avoid penalising for spelling errors/sloppy papers/penmanship

❏ Make activity/questions open-ended

❏ Require student to defend answers

❏ Assign independent projects which teach planning and research skills at higher level

❏ Provide long distance learning & tiered assignments

❏ Other...

Self management – follow through

❏ Visual daily schedule

❏ Calendars

❏ Check often for understanding/review

❏ Request parental reinforcement

❏ Have students repeat directions

❏ Teach study skills

❏ Use study sheets to organise material

❏ Plan for generalisation

❏ Provide & match mentor with student's interest/talent

❏ Develop teacher/student written contract

❏ Other...

Testing adaptations

❏ Oral

❏ Taped

❏ Read test to student

☐ Preview language of test

☐ Short answer

☐ Multiple choice

☐ Modify format

☐ Shorten length of questions

☐ Extended time frame

☐ Test administered individually

☐ Integrate test skills into required projects or products

☐ Other..

Motivation and Reinforcement

☐ Verbal

☐ Non-verbal

☐ Positive reinforcement

☐ Concrete reinforcement

☐ Planned motivating sequences of activities

☐ Reinforce initiation

☐ Offer choice

☐ Use strengths/interests often

☐ Allow students to 'buy' time for advanced work

☐ Provide a mentor for.............................

(Adapted from North East Independent School District of San Antonio, Texas, by IRCA 10/92 and reproduced with kind permission from the author.)

Chapter Six

Programme delivery and accountability

How do they do it and how do we know they are doing it well?

Movesville School for the kinetic learner

chris fox

Teacher: "I think I'm doing a good job"

Programme delivery

The Learning Resource Centre programme is defined as the provision that is made for the children who need extra support in their learning. This includes all documents used in the programme *eg* referral, assessment, standardised testing, IEPs and reporting as well as resource materials. The LRC programme should also include a philosophy statement that is in line with the school mission statement and which could be placed in the LRC Policy and Curriculum Guide as well as in the school policy manual. The school mission statement should make a reference to children with learning differences and make it perfectly clear that these children are welcomed into the school. Having a philosophy statement also makes the aims of the department clearer as it is essential that all members of staff implement the aims in the same way. The LRC Policy and Curriculum Guide should also include a list of resources used in the department.

The LRC programme should be broad enough to:

- support the children in gaining access to the school curriculum;
- allow children to develop their potential;
- provide enough resources, materials and LRC library available to all staff and parents;
- provide in-service for:

    a) classroom teachers to support the child who has learning differences in their class;

    b) classroom teachers to offer enrichment and acceleration for the child who has been identified as gifted and talented;

    c) aiding teachers to deal with emotional and behaviour problems within the classroom;

    d) aiding teachers in how to deal with children with ADHD within the classroom;

    e) aiding the head and teachers in how to read student cumulative files, psychological reports and how to read Wechsler Intelligence Scale profiles and other tests;

    f) aiding parents in how to deal with their children who receive learning support.

It is important for the school's head to attend all the in-service sessions (a-f) in order to give support to the LRC programme and to show that the LRC is supported from the top.

Teacher delivery

But what about the teachers who are working with Special Needs students? How can these teachers be effective? Given that they have all the resources they need (unlikely), sometimes have to make themselves unpopular in the best interest of their students (usually), often have to teach in corridors or broom cupboards (likely) … how do we keep them sparky and motivated or rather, how do they keep themselves sparky and motivated?

Pfiffner (1996, p164), in her book *All About ADHD: The Complete Practical Guide for Classroom Teachers*, clearly states:

> 'Don't neglect your emotional needs and don't count on the students to meet your emotional needs. Have outlets for re-energising: exercise regularly, consult with colleagues and never ever lose your sense of humour!
>
> 1. Set small goals for yourself and reward yourself every step of the way. It is a tough job that you have chosen, be nice to yourself!
>
> 2. Get help from other professionals. No one has all the answers. Set up a support system with your colleagues.
>
> 3. Expect that you will have bad days. Do not feel guilty… it could be worse; there could be eight days in a week!

4. Expect that students will have setbacks and separate yourself from them.

5. Don't give up!'

Student delivery

The ethos of a school is extremely important in giving children the confidence to succeed and develop their own potential. When differences are accepted, valued and respected, schools become happier places.

Using students' strengths to help develop the skills of other students is well known in many schools and one of the many examples of this is when children with very specific learning disabilities are included in the mainstream classroom. At this point, our definitions become too specific and by referring to these children as having 'specific learning disabilities', we are referring to those children who have been diagnosed with, for example, Downs' syndrome, brain injury, cerebral palsy *etc*: that is those children who are generally not accepted into international schools.

In certain international schools around the world, programmes have been established to include these students in the mainstream and to provide them with a rich programme to meet their individual needs. Inclusion is the norm as these children's educational needs are met in the same way as any other child's. The benefits to the child with specific disabilities are obvious: good behaviour models, improved language stimulation, social interaction *etc*.

These are all learned from other students. Students taking the International Baccalaureate Diploma are required to spend time giving service to others as part of the Creative Action and Service (CAS) module of their programme. The CAS student can become an important role model in the life of these children and can take a very active part in the delivery of the child's individual educational programme. Not many teachers can teach a student how to be 'cool' and yet to a CAS student this is second nature! They are excellent social models, particularly for developmentally-delayed students who are teenagers but are being treated as young children by their parents.

Similarly, the child in the mainstream benefits enormously from working with other students in this way. If we are to educate students for the future, tolerance, acceptance and accommodation are skills that we want our students to develop. By including all students we are offering our children the chance to experience human diversity and to accept it as the norm. In fact, the ideal international school is one in which all students are accepted and are able to have their educational needs met.

The child who is gifted and talented can also be integrated into the mainstream and can also have their needs met. Their specific talents can be demonstrated and they can also be role models for other children. In an environment that encourages all children, this is not classed as 'showing off' but rather as applauding talents which are obvious.

The child who has dyslexia or any other 'labelled' difficulty, certainly has strengths in other areas, and it is up to the teacher to ensure that these strengths are built upon. This not only enhances the child's self esteem, an important pre-requisite for learning success, but also allows all children to be successful in their own eyes and in the eyes of their peers. If these strengths can be utilised to help their peers, that is even better. Again, create an environment where all children are accepted for their differences and provide them with the opportunities to excel. Use the students to deliver the programme of instruction and to work with their peers in a team or cooperative group. These skills are life skills and ones that are becoming more and more important.

NB: **TEAM** – **T**ogether **E**ach **A**chieves **M**ore.

Scheduling

There are no hard and fast rules as to when the support lessons should be scheduled, as this is obviously very dependent on the needs of the children. The variables to consider are:

- Will the child benefit more from gaining support within the classroom environment or by being withdrawn for specific lessons?

- If the child were withdrawn for lessons, would she benefit more from being in the classroom at that time? Is she missing a music lesson but is good at music and could be successful?

- How can the resources of the department be used in the most efficient way? Can children with similar needs be grouped?

If children were receiving learning support within the classroom environment, the person delivering that support should submit classroom IEPs for the children in coordination with the child's regular class teacher. It is too easy for a support teacher to walk into the classroom each day, unsupervised, and never plan (see Chapter 4, *Organisation, services and personnel* for a job description for a Classroom Support teacher). To avoid this, the LRC coordinator should create a 'Request for LRC classroom support form'. The request should cover, for example, the following areas:

- reasons for classroom support for a particular student;

- responsibilities of the LRC teacher;

- subject and resources to be used;

- how many periods weekly and on which days.

When the completed form has been processed, the classroom teacher should work with the LRC support teacher to create a Classroom Support IEP. Copies of the Classroom IEPs should be kept in (1) the regular classroom, (2) by the LRC teacher, and (3) in the child's file held in the LRC. By formalising classroom support other teachers, the head, the child and the parents can see what is actually happening during the regular classroom hours.

Materials

As far as possible, support teachers should try to use familiar classroom materials to the student in their remediation/enrichment programmes. This makes the learning more meaningful and stops the child from feeling isolated. Similarly, if a child were withdrawn for individual support, there should not be the expectation that the child 'catches up' on the classroom work that has been missed. This places an unfair burden on the child and defeats the object of the extra support.

Individual Educational Plan

Once the child's needs have been evaluated an Individual Educational Plan should be formulated which will outline the student's goals.

Writing an Individual Educational Plan (IEP) is an art. It is almost like learning a new language while writing a lot in very small spaces. Therefore, when writing up an IEP, it is essential to keep in mind the following components:

1. the present levels of educational achievement/performance of the student;

2. the specific individualised learning outcomes set for that student for that school year, excluding goals that would normally be expected at age-grade level as prescribed in local guidebooks;

3. any required adaptations to educational materials, and instructional and assessment methods designed to accommodate the student's needs;

4. any support services that are provided to facilitate meeting the student's needs;

5. a description of the place where the educational programme is to be provided;

6. the names of all personnel who will be providing the educational programme and the support services;

7. the period of time over which the IEP will be in effect and the process for reviewing and evaluating the success of the IEP. (Brock & Griffin 2000, p191).

It is important that all individuals involved with the student, including the student and his/her parents, agree with the items written in the IEP and frequently evaluate whether the goals have been effective.

How de we know if we are successful?

Simple... are the children making progress? Certainly, this is the aim of any intervention. However, look at the programme with the following points in mind:

• Have I been flexible in adapting the programme to meet the needs of the child?

• Is the child relaxed and confident when I teach him?

• Do I communicate clearly with the parents?

• Is my record keeping adequate and up to date?

• Do I communicate with the child's classroom teacher?

• Have I supported the child, not only in reaching academic goals but in developing his self-esteem?

• Have I used a multi-sensory approach to achieve the goal?

- Has the child progressed?
- How have I assessed/measured progress?

Clearly, the programme should be continually reviewed and updated and the best support teacher, as with any teacher, is one who is continually reflecting on their practice and evaluating the needs of their students.

Reporting to parents

Once a programme has been put in place, there should be regular reports on the developments within the programme. Most schools give a written report to parents twice a year and also have a number of Parent Evenings and home school contact procedures.

If a child has very specific needs that require an individual programme, the parents should be kept closely involved with the progress their child makes and informed of any changes in the programme.

The LRC should send home a report that accompanies the classroom report but also write reports that are more frequent, as goals will be achieved in between these bi-annual reports. A communication notebook is also an excellent way of maintaining regular contact with parents and one that develops an excellent relationship between the home and school. Parents are kept informed on either a daily or weekly basis of anything that is pertinent to their child's learning programme. The parent is also invited to comment and relate any relevant information regarding anything that may be happening at home. This is extremely helpful to the teacher, by giving another perspective on the child's learning. It also serves to emphasise the crucial role played by the parents in understanding and supporting their child's needs.

Meetings with parents are also a very necessary part of the LRC programme, as these give a chance for both parties, the home and the school, to discuss concerns, developments, progress and to share examples of the child's learning. We would suggest that these take place both on the school Parent Evening and also throughout the school year, as it is essential that parents are aware of all aspects of their child's programme.

Keep it simple

The most important thing to remember when writing a report is that it must be comprehensible for the parents. Very often, English may not be the native language of the parent and so if many 'jargon' or 'specialised' words are used, the parent may be completely confused. Use plain English to describe the progress and do not try to impress the parent with your knowledge of long words! Educational jargon can be incomprehensible even for English mother tongue speakers and can alienate parents.

What type of curriculum and how do we ensure that the child is receiving exactly what he requires to reach his potential?

Effective learning support implies that each child will be given the support that is needed to learn to the best of their ability. It implies that we do not put ceilings on children's potential but rather allow them to go as far as they can go. So if we provide this, what type of curriculum should be in place to allow them to do this?

How is 'curriculum' defined? By definition, curriculum is everything that takes place within the school community and not just a syllabus of subjects to be taught and specific knowledge benchmarks to be attained. It includes the school ethos and the respect that there is between teacher and pupil, parent and teacher, teacher and teacher. If effective learning support is to be provided, the school should have the means whereby children have the necessary support to develop their own potential within a curriculum that allows for different learning styles and promotes higher levels of thinking.

The child that is merely to attain a certain mark on a test can be coached to pass that test but the child who is asked to use their intelligence in a variety of ways and is asked to take more responsibility for their own learning has no ceiling for their own performance. A curriculum that promotes self-reliance, communication, independent learning *etc*, is one that is more accessible to children with learning differences than a curriculum that consists of a syllabus of benchmarks to be achieved.

So how do we provide effective learning support?

1. Look at your curriculum: does it allow the child to really develop their potential or does it provide benchmarks, which can only be attained by some?

2. Do you have enough support teachers for your children? If not, are the teachers sensitised to children with differing needs?

3. Have you provided opportunities for the parents to be involved in the education of their children? Do they know how to develop their child's potential?

4. Do you offer support to parents?

5. Are you honest with the parents? Do you have straightforward policies that 'tell it how it is'?

6. Have you got enough testing materials so that you can identify the children's needs? If you have, can you use them properly?

7. Do you really want, *really* want, to have children in your school who will require extra support? This is a rhetorical question and one that will hopefully make you reflect on how you relate to children with different needs.

In spreading a wide identification net over the student population at international schools, the following programmes, which have been proven successful, should be considered when developing a curriculum for students with Special Needs in the regular and LRC classroom setting. It is recognised that there are many more excellent programmes at international schools. However, the ones outlined here have been observed in use and are worthy of consideration, and most of which can be used within the regular classroom with all students. In line with the Optimal Match Concept, the programmes are designed to bring out the gifts and talents of all students in a variety of different means while providing various outlets for Special Needs students to shine.

A selection of effective programmes

Schoolwide Enrichment Model

There are extensive writings about the Schoolwide Enrichment Model and some of these writings are listed in Appendix E, *Resources*. An overview of the Schoolwide Enrichment Model created by Renzulli and Reis (1986) shows a one-page summary of the model, and it would help to read over this page to have a sense of how the programme is structured.

Drs Renzulli and Reis direct The National Research Center on the Gifted and Talented located at the University of Connecticut. Their Schoolwide Enrichment Model (SEM) can be found at:

<http://www.gifted.uconn.edu/sempage.html> (17 June 2002).

The site includes articles, present practices survey, research and evaluation, curriculum guides, and SEM resources. Renzulli and Reis (1994), published the extensive research related to the Schoolwide Enrichment Model in the *Gifted Child Quarterly*. For an update on the research since 1994, please contact Sally Reis at: The National Research Center on the Gifted and Talented School of Education, University of Connecticut, Storrs, Connecticut 06269-3007, US. Phone: 001-860-486-0618.

Instead of writing a typical description of Renzulli & Reis' *Schoolwide Enrichment Model*, the authors have included a proposal, which was created for an international school by Dr Ulrike Stedtnitz in 1985 (see below).

Proposal for a programme to encourage creative-productive (gifted) behaviour in children at an international school

Programme goals

The programme, which will be based on the well-known and thoroughly field-tested Enrichment Triad Model (Renzulli, University of Connecticut), is designed to enrich the educational environment for all children and to specifically nurture gifted behaviour. Gifted behaviour has been defined as the interaction between above-average ability in any one area, task commitment and creativity, brought to bear upon an area of intense personal interest such as astronomy, photography, physics, music, leadership, journalism, history, *etc*.

Students will be motivated in a variety of ways to do independent or group projects (Type III activities). These activities have the following specific objectives:

- To provide opportunities in which students can apply their interests, knowledge, creative ideas, and task-commitment to a self-selected problem or area of study.

- To acquire advanced level understanding of the knowledge (content) and methodology (process) that are used within particular disciplines, artistic areas of expression, and interdisciplinary studies.

- To develop authentic products that are primarily directed toward bringing about a desired impact upon an appropriate audience.

- To develop self-directed learning skills in the areas of planning, organisation, resource utilization, time management, decision-making, and self-evaluation.

- To develop task commitment, self-confidence, feelings of creative accomplishment, and the ability to interact effectively with older students, teachers, and persons with advanced levels of interest and expertise in a common area of involvement.

Brief description of the programme

The programme will consist of talent identification for all students, staff training and implementation of the Enrichment Triad Model (Renzulli, 1977) in all classrooms. This model is very flexible and well suited to the needs of an international student body.

The programme will feature two major components: Compacting for students, where necessary, and Type I, II, and III activities. Compacting refers to the elimination of unnecessary skill training for students advanced in language or maths, and substitution of more difficult and challenging work.

Who will benefit from the programme

All students of the international school, including learning disabled children with high abilities and bright underachievers. A very high percentage of children at an international school show above-average abilities in one or several areas. Because of this fact, the new programme promises to be particularly worthwhile. All children will participate in the Type I and Type II components of the programme, and about 10% of all children will be involved in the Type III component of the programme initially. That percentage might gradually increase.

Programme duration

Throughout the school year, for a testing period of at least two years.

Staffing

All teachers (Grades K-6) will be involved in the programme (classroom teachers will be responsible for Type I and Type II components, as well as participate in Individualised Educational Planning).

The learning resource room teacher will facilitate the Type III activities.

The school psychologist will assist with talent identification as well as Individualised Educational Planning (IEPs).

The programme consultant will be responsible for programme planning, staff training and evaluation of the programme, with the help of the school staff.

Curriculum compacting: what it means

Definition

Modifying or 'streamlining' the regular curriculum in order to:

- eliminate repetition of previously mastered material;

- upgrade the challenge level of the regular classroom;

- provide time for appropriate enrichment and/or acceleration activities while ensuring mastery of basic skills.

Objectives

- To create a challenging learning environment within the context of the regular classroom;
- To guarantee proficiency in the basis curriculum;
- To 'buy' time for enrichment and acceleration.

Advantages

- Modification of the regular curriculum through an assessment of student strengths;
- Elimination or acceleration of skills activities in strength areas following assessment;
- Systematic planning of enrichment and/or acceleration activities to replace skills already mastered or can master at a faster pace.

(Stedtnitz, 1985).

The Steps Toward Curriculum Compacting (Reis, Burns, & Renzulli, 1990) have been added here as a further explanation of this topic:

Step One: Identify the relevant learning objectives in a particular subject area or grade level.

Step Two: Identify students who may possess prior mastery of these objectives.

Step Three: Develop some means of pre-testing students on one or more of these objectives prior to instruction.

Step Four: Administer pre-tests to students and determine their level of mastery prior to instruction.

Step Five: Streamline practice, drill or instructional time for students who have demonstrated prior mastery of these objectives.

Step Six: Provide individualised instructional options for students who have not yet mastered all of the objectives that were pre-tested but are capable of mastering these objectives more quickly than other classmates.

Step Seven: Suggest enrichment or acceleration options for students who have demonstrated prior mastery of these learning objectives.

Step Eight: Maintain formal or informal records of this process and the instructional options available to 'compacted' students.

Differentiated instruction

Theresa Cullen, Differentiation Specialist for the Highly Able at The American School of the Hague, has written a document to describe what programmes her school is providing for the highly able from grades 2-8:

Differentiated instructional specialist – elementary school
The differentiation specialist works with both teachers and students in elementary grades 2-4. The specialist works with teachers to differentiate cur-

riculum in order to meet the varying needs of students. This entails planning lessons, differentiating materials, selecting appropriate literature and modelling strategies and lessons in the classroom. It also entails looking at the individual needs of a student and designing appropriate educational plans for the individual.

In order to deliver this differentiated curriculum, the specialist works with students in a variety of ways: individually, in small groups, and within the whole class.

For individual students whose needs go beyond the differentiated classroom, a team (consisting of the counsellor, differentiation specialist, principal, teachers and parents) meets to decide on an appropriate Individual Education Plan using various methodologies including the following: curriculum compacting; individual or small group investigations; subject acceleration; grade skipping; and finally, working in the resource room. The resource room is where smaller, defined homogeneous groups work. This currently occurs in grades 2, 3 and 4 in the academic areas of language arts and mathematics.

As a basis for our highly-able language arts curriculum, we use the Language Arts Program for High-Ability Learners developed by the Center for Gifted Education at the College of William and Mary in Williamsburg, Virginia. We also work with the Renzulli Schoolwide Enrichment Model and specifically, the Schoolwide Reading Enrichment Model designed by Reis, Gubbins, Richards from the University of Connecticut. Our current third and fourth grade enrichment mathematics program is a combination of the Everyday Mathematics Program from the University of Chicago, the Stock Market Project sponsored by Securities Industry Foundation for Economic Education (SIFEE), and The Math Forum On-Line Problem Solving sponsored by Drexel University.

To determine which students would benefit from the enrichment room, a variety of assessments are used. As a basis for the reading program, a student must demonstrate two years or more above grade level in the area of comprehension. This is determined by use of a variety of instruments including the Rigby Benchmarking Assessment: used by classroom teachers to determine reading levels. After a student demonstrates this reading level, a classroom teacher will then make a recommendation for further testing. Further testing instruments include The Degrees of Reading Power (DRP) used to determine comprehension. In addition, the Stanford Series 9 Examination is given to third and fourth grade students in the spring of each year. This is an additional source of information regarding a student's potential. For mathematics, again teacher input helps to identify potential students. Classroom pre-testing of units and year-long curriculum helps teachers in identifying mathematical aptitude. Additionally, score reports from the Stanford examination are used as well as the TOMGAS Test for Mathematical Giftedness.

Elementary school enrichment programs offered at ASH

- Odyssey of the mind;
- Chess club;

- Performing arts: grade level musical productions;
- Visual arts: visual art fair;
- Foreign language: Dutch;
- Physical education;
- Technology.

Differentiated instructional specialist – middle school

For highly able students in grades 5 to 8, an inclusive approach to differentiating instruction is used by having the teachers and the specialist collaborate in order to meet the needs of students.

This occurs in several ways including the creation of differentiated curriculum, the development of special units or projects and by selecting appropriate materials. A variety of instructional approaches are also applied. Typically, this includes working within the classroom with individuals or small groups. Additionally, small or individualised instruction may occur outside of the classroom.

Identifying a student's needs and potential

Using a variety of data, teacher input and classroom observations evidence is gathered in order to better understand a student's needs and potential. Several different assessment pieces are used to gather data on individual students and groups. This helps to determine a student's ability and to also determine a student's growth over the course of the year. In addition to placement, this helps to match appropriate materials with a student's ability and potential. This also helps in the planning and implementation of lessons, units and projects.

For individual students whose needs go beyond the differentiated classroom, a team (consisting of the counsellor, differentiation specialist, principal and/or dean of students, teachers and parents) meets to decide on an appropriate Individual Education Plan using various methodologies including the following: curriculum compacting; individual or small group investigations; subject acceleration; grade skipping; on-line course work; and mentorship.

Additional programming

The specialist, in conjunction with Johns Hopkins University's Center for Gifted Education located in the United States, is working to provide students with exceptional abilities (in the areas of mathematics, humanities, science and computer) the opportunity to participate in various programmes offered by the university. These include on-line correspondence courses and summer school courses. Additionally, ASH recognises those students who apply to the University to participate in the annual International Talent Search at grades 7 and 8. Selection for the various programs is based on selection criteria proposed by the University. The assessments that determine placement are administered at ASH. The University is fully responsible for the assessment scoring and placement criterion. A student who is selected and who is interested in participating in the program will then apply directly to the university.

Middle school enrichment programs offered at ASH

- Odyssey of the mind;
- Chess club;
- Sports intramurals and team sports;
- The performing arts: drama, dance, instrumental music, and musical productions;
- The visual arts;
- Foreign language offerings – French, Spanish, Dutch;
- Technology;
- Johns Hopkins University International Talent Search – Grades 7 and 8;
- Johns Hopkins University summer programs.

(email communication, Theresa Cullen, March 2003).

CTY international talent search

The Centre for Talented Youth, Johns Hopkins University Maryland (CTY) promotes a yearly International Talent Search for students. The search 'is designed to identify, assess, and recognise students with exceptional mathematical and/or verbal reasoning abilities' from grades 7-8 and highly exceptional grade 6 students. The International Talent Search invites students who have scored at or above the 97th percentile on a nationally standardised aptitude or achievement test, such as an ERB test, to take the SAT I, a more difficult test with a higher ceiling. The SAT I provides highly able students with information that can validate their exceptional mathematical and verbal abilities, and encourages the development of their academic strengths. The SAT I is administered worldwide in major cities or at international school sites one of more times during the year.

On page 163 in Appendix D, *Case Studies* please refer to a story about 'Laura' to illustrate how students may benefit from entering the CTY International Talent Search. CTY's summer courses and distance learning programmes are similar to the CTYI described below. To apply for the search, request an application form from CTY at CTY Headquarters, CTY International Talent Search, The Johns Hopkins University, 3400 N. Charles Street, Baltimore, MD 21218, USA. Alternatively, e-mail: ctyinfo@jhu.edu or log on to the CTY website: <http://www.jhu.edu/gifted>.

Of interest to our European readers is the CTYI, located in Dublin, Ireland. CTYI has been modelled from CTY Baltimore at The Johns Hopkins University. CTYI accommodates over 2,000 students aged 8-16 years annually. About 20% of its summer students come from overseas. CTYI provides assessments, Saturday classes, summer programmes and correspondence courses in over 60 academic areas ranging from archaeology, astronomy and architecture to literature, philosophy, politics and pharmacology. For more information about CTYI, log onto their website: <http://www.dcu.ie/ctyi/> or e-mail: ctyi@dcu.ie

Interest inventories

Getting students to complete interest inventories can obtain much information about the student's interests at home as well as at school. One effective interest inventory is, *The Interest-A-Lyzer* (Renzulli, 1977), see Appendix E, *Resources*. This inventory has been used to make a survey of like-minded students and group them to work on common interests in an independent study environment within the regular classroom and on an individual basis in the LRC. Another effective interest inventory is 'My Way...An Expression Style Inventory' (Kettle, Renzulli, and Rizza, 1998) which was published in the *Gifted Child Quarterly*, 42 (1) Winter 1998. This inventory has also been used in the regular classroom and in the resource room and has proven effective for profiling students' interests in ten different areas.

After students complete an interest inventory, it is recommended that teachers set up ways to help students further develop their interests. Dr Susan Baum lists ten ways that might help students develop interests:

- Enlist community resources to act as mentors.

- Set up lunch dates with adults who have similar interests.

- Create class experts and allow them to give a demonstration lesson or presentation about their interest.

- Create interest development centres.

- Implement WIBA (What I'm Best At) time in your classroom once or twice a week. Group students by what they are most interested in or best at. Have them develop group projects or explore interests together.

- Offer mini-courses or study groups in the areas of common student interests.

- Integrate student interests and strengths into the regular curriculum.

- Find peers with common interests through computer bulletin boards.

- Offer opportunities for independent study.

- Display your enthusiasm for the students' interests by asking questions, clipping articles, or bringing in books about the topic of interest. In short, if you see anything that would augment a student's interest, find time to share it.

> (Baum, Susan (1996). *Nurturing Talents and Interests of Students*. Lecture given at the Optimal Match Network Institute)

It is useful to add to the Student Enrolment/Application Form to include the nature of the parents' interests, professions, and expertise in different areas. That way, schools can find a talent pool from which students might find mentors, and/or parents could come to the school to give lectures about their areas of expertise. An interest survey of staff, on which they could also list their areas of expertise and interests, would also be of use. Staff could be invited to give a mini-lecture series and be assigned as student mentors.

Independent study

Independent study does not mean sending the student to the library with the assignment to produce an independent study. A student who is designated to work on an independent study needs to have a structured approach to the study guided by the teacher or Learning Resource teacher. Independent studies may form a basis for all students in a particular classroom to learn research skills and where all students can go as far as they can according to their own potential. The following is a project, which was introduced in the fifth grade to all students.

Introduction to Independent Study Project (Haldimann & Wegelin in 1993 continuing yearly to 2003)

This project, by Doherty and Evans (1989) see Appendix E, *Resources*, is designed to encourage creative-productive behaviour through the use of enrichment activities for individual and group work within the classroom. All the students will participate in the pilot project two classroom periods per week and be expected to produce and present a product to complete the project. All students will learn skills necessary for success in school:

- ability to think independently;
- to ask meaningful questions;
- to take notes;
- to interact socially.

The teacher will give the student the responsibility for her/his own learning and help the student to learn good research habits. The teacher will also be able to help identify students who are potentially academically talented through their process and products from the independent study.

Objectives

The Special Education resource teachers and the Educational Psychologist will aid the fifth grade teacher to guide the students to:

- Engage in opportunities in which students can apply their knowledge, interests, creative ideas to self-selected areas of independent study;
- Develop self-directed learning skills in areas of planning, organisation, critical and creative thinking, resource utilization, time management, decision making, and self-evaluation;
- Develop task commitment, self-confidence, pride in creative accomplishment, and ability to interact effectively with their fellow students and teachers;
- Create authentic products to be demonstrated to a select audience.

The students will be guided through the following nine steps taken from the *Self-Starter Kit*

For *Independent Study* (1989) see Appendix E, *Resources*:

Step One: The student selects a topic that is issue-oriented.

Step Two: The student establishes a schedule.

Step Three: The student develops five or more questions (first objectives) to direct his research.

Step Four: The student secures references and seeks sources of raw data.

Step Five: The student researches the topic, collects raw data, and takes notes.

Step Six: The student develops five final objectives using Bloom's taxonomy.

Step Seven: The student has a conference with the teacher who evaluates the depth of knowledge and idea production.

Step Eight: The student makes a product showing some of his new ideas.

Step Nine: The student's product is displayed, evaluated with a friend, and examined by an expert.

Resource materials

1. Doherty, Edith J S & Evans, Louise C (1989). *Self-Starter Kit for Independent Study*. Connecticut: Synergetics.

2. Teacher and Student Created Evaluation Forms

Evaluation

The pilot project will be evaluated as to the quality of student projects, student enthusiasm for continuing the project, and teacher, student, and head evaluation of project design and outcomes. If deemed successful, the project will be expanded to include the third and fourth grade classes and into the lower and upper school the following year. The type of enrichment planned will help identify gifted and talent students and allow all students in the classes to participate in projects according to their ability.

Authors' comments

The *Self-Starter Kit* was revised and updated in 2000 and the *Primary Independent Study and Student Book* was revised and updated in 1998 at Synergetics Press (see Appendix E, *Resources,* Synergetics Press co-ordinates several other resources for independent study).

Oral communication

Although many schools provide forums for students to give speeches, the John F Kennedy International School in Switzerland goes a step further. Oral communication is a structured approach to speech writing and production, which is guided by a step-by-step process from a written curriculum within the school's language arts programme.

Oral communication encourages all students at the school (grades 2-8) to participate in presenting speeches. As a result it helps teachers in accommodating students with exceptional talents as well as encouraging those with learning disabilities and/or ADHD to write, memorise and perform. Oral communication is another avenue to pursue in enriching all students. The programme has proven to be a confidence-building exercise for students and an excellent way of teaching students to organise their ideas and to practice expressing them effectively. Students, parents and friends are invited to an oral communications day to hear the presentations of all the class champions.

Students in grades 5 to 8 each prepare a three-to-five minute presentation. Grades 3 and 4, plus any students new to the English language, are expected to speak for a minimum of two minutes on a topic of interest to them. Younger students also have an opportunity to participate in the speech-making process and are asked to choose a favourite poem, short story or short passage to memorise and to practice speaking with expression.

Students discuss with their teachers how to prepare an effective oral presentation. Parental support is enlisted by providing parents with a short document *Keys to Effective Oral Presentations*, which may help them assist their children. Student peers as well as adults are involved in the evaluation of the speakers

Invention convention

Finally, one more programme, which has proved to be successful, is the 'Invention Convention', developed by the elementary section of an international school. Again, this is a structured approach and students are not just asked to invent something and bring it to school to show the class. All children are instructed about what inventions are and how people have contributed to the world with their own inventions. Invention units are prepared by the teachers, and the students who are already entranced by this concept are instructed to construct their own inventions with guidance from the teacher. The final result is for students in each class to present their inventions to their peers and to another class in the school. The three best inventions from each class are also presented to the high school students and parents.

Authors' comments

There are so many good programmes, which are practised in international schools that the time is ripe for the establishment of an Internet-based international school resource site where schools can share successful programmes.

Learning disabilities

The following books (complete ordering information is listed in Appendix E, *Resources*) provide enough teaching strategies to start a successful programme. The books, which have been written by Dr Melvin Levine, incorporate:

- *A Mind at A Time*
- *All Kinds of Minds*
- *Developmental Variation and Learning Disorders*
- *Keeping a head in School*

The following books are listed in full in Appendix E, *Resources*:

- *Dyslexia: A Teaching Handbook* (specific learning disabilities)
- *Mathematics for Dyslexics: A Teaching Handbook* (specific learning disabilities)
- *How to Detect and Manage Dyslexia* (specific learning disabilities)
- *No Easy Answers* (excellent for elementary LD students)
- *Succeeding Against The Odds* (excellent for high school LD students)
- *Overcoming Dyslexia: A New and Complete Science-Based Program for Overcoming Reading Problems at Any Level* (by Sally Shaywitz, 2003, this book has had rave reviews in describing the causes of dyslexia and proscribing programmes to treat different types of dyslexia.)

The Wilson Reading System

The Wilson Reading System teaches students the structure of words and language through a carefully sequenced, 12-step programme that helps them master decoding and spelling (encoding) in English. The system allows the student to learn cumulatively and systematically, and students can move forward from success to success.

Originally designed for adults and students in grades 5-12, the Wilson Reading System has been revised for use with elementary students as well. Wilson Reading System materials feature two separate vocabulary levels; Level A vocabulary is suitable for elementary students, ESL students and older students with limited vocabularies, while Level B is appropriate for students beyond elementary grades, with more advanced vocabularies. The Wilson Reading System can be used for one-to-one tutoring or in small groups. The system can be used within the regular classroom environment or to students within a LRC. (Please see Appendix E, *Resources* for additional information.)

Authors' comments

This programme is excellent and has been observed to work well with students with specific language disabilities (dyslexia). The system is organised so students as well as their teachers can chart their progress.

Modifications for language

When a student is having difficulty with reading:

- make sure hearing and vision have been checked;
- modify the student's reading material;
- outline reading material for the student;
- tape record reading material for the student to listen to while reading the printed text;
- arrange for a peer tutor to read or study with the student;
- provide the student with a quiet place to read;
- have the student paraphrase material orally;
- reduce the emphasis on competition;
- give the student time to read a selection more than once;
- supplement books with multimedia materials;
- prepare student for reading by relating what s/he already knows to new vocabulary;
- make a reading window for textbook use. Student moves window down and across page while reading;
- suggest the student use context clues to identify unfamiliar words or phrases;
- vary reading material to include high interest selections from magazines and newspapers;
- use students' dictated stories for reading;
- develop a word finder for students to record unfamiliar words with a picture or contextual clues;
- identify a peer to whom the student may turn for help;
- label objects in the classroom to help student associate words with tangible aspects of their environment;
- assess student's interest in order to identify reading material;
- make reading materials easily accessible to the student in the classroom;
- encourage interest in reading by having students share books with friends;
- have student read lower grade level stories to younger children;
- include predictable books in the class library;
- be sensitive to any reading situations which might make a student uncomfortable (reading aloud in a group, *etc*);
- provide assistance to student in finding reading material according to ability and interest. Seek books from authors that are popular with the student;
- offer membership to paperback book clubs.

When the student is having difficulty with writing:

- change the format of the materials from which the student copies;
- use a frame or window to cover all material except what is to be copied;
- have a peer assist the student in copying;
- make sure student proofreads his/her work;
- state clearly the expectations between a first draft and revisions;
- encourage students to use peer conferencing when proofreading;
- have student write a daily journal;
- make sure the student knows why s/he is learning spelling words (give a concrete example of how the word can be used in student's life);
- make sure that spelling words are those the student uses on a routine basis.

(Sally Reis, 2000, reprinted with kind permission of the author)

Reis and McGuire (2000) have studied high ability students with learning disabilities who succeeded in postsecondary education. The authors concluded that the compensation strategies were slightly different for each participant in the study but found common elements including: 'multiple learning strategies, the use of carefully selected and individually necessary compensation strategies, and the integration of certain executive functions that guided the students'.

Unfortunately, the students reported that they did not have the type of learning support in their elementary and secondary school that they found at the university level. They were not taught compensation strategies either in the learning disability and/or gifted programmes and reported that self-advocacy and self-reliance was not taught which were a critical factor in higher education. The authors recommend that elementary and secondary schools examine their programmes and take into account what university level students reported as the most important factors which helped them succeed at the university level.

Federation of American Women's Clubs Overseas (FAWCO)

During the annual conference of the Federation of American Women's Clubs Overseas (FAWCO) in Stockholm, Sweden, March 27 – April 1, 2003, the Educational Support Committee (ESC), presented the results of its two-year project to support mainstream classroom teachers worldwide. The project was created by Susan van Alsenoy, chair of the FAWCO ESC and member of the American Women's Club of Antwerp, who is currently working in learning support at the Antwerp British School. By researching simple strategies that pre-school through university professors can employ to help LD (learning differently/learning disabled) students in their classes, the ESC hope to make learning more rewarding for teachers and students alike. It has been estimated that 15% of the students in every class learn via techniques not usually employed in most mainstream classrooms.

The ESC has previously produced a report aimed at providing help to internationally-mobile LD students, their families and their educational professionals. This study, *Students Who Learn Differently*, can be found at <http://studentswholearn.fawco.org>. It is available for free in the public sector of the FAWCO site, and it has been speech-enabled for those with reading difficulties.

The project

Because most mainstream teachers throughout the world receive little or no practical guidance on how to help LD students in their classrooms, and because most mainstream teachers are very busy people who work many uncompensated hours, the FAWCO ESC has prepared a very simple one-page guide of strategies that they should find easy to implement in their classrooms with relatively small changes to their current teaching style. This project does not give a detailed explanation of learning difficulties. Additional pages contain references for teachers who would like to pursue the topic. It is suggested that teachers keep the project sheet together with their class register for easy reference.

These suggestions have been collected and refined over a two-year period by Special Needs specialists all over the world. The 78 FAWCO member clubs have been asked to translate the project paper into their host country languages. In addition to disseminating this information within their clubs, they will be asked to make it available to persons involved in education in their countries. A copy of the translations will be made available for free on the ESC section of the FAWCO website. Anyone wishing to offer a translation, FAWCO member or not, is asked to contact esc@fawco.org.

LD support for teachers worldwide (FAWCO 2003)

The following list of suggestions and strategies has been created to support all teachers in their efforts to teach students who learn differently better and more effectively. The ideas have been taken from the work of experts in the field of LD (learning differences/specific learning disabilities) the world over, and they are of benefit to all students, not just those with LD. Sources and participants who endorse the results of this project are acknowledged on the following pages.

General considerations

1. Teachers are urged to re-examine the notion of what is 'fair.' 'Fair' does not mean that every student gets the same treatment, but that every student gets what he or she needs. LD is a neurological condition that is beyond the control of the individual. This student is more normal than different, and different does not mean defective. There are degrees of LD, mild, moderate and severe. It might go undiagnosed as late as secondary school, university, or even never at all.

2. The younger the child is diagnosed, the more often remediation is possible. When a student is older, you should deal more with coping strategies and self-advocacy skills.

3. There are different kinds of intelligence and different learning styles. It is usually the students who have good linguistic, logical and mathematical abilities who are the most successful in school. However other types of intelligence, such as musical, environmental, spiritual, bodily-kinesthetic, interpersonal, spatial, and intrapersonal are also valuable, and add much to the knowledge and enjoyment of life. These intelligences also need to be recognised and educated.

4. Learning is best when brought through the modalities of hearing, sight, touch and movement – multi-sensory teaching. Most students retain 10% of what they read, 20% of what they hear, 30% of what they see, 50% of what they see and hear, 70% of what they say, and 90% of what they say and do. A cumulative, highly-structured, sequential approach, which uses multi-sensory materials and software, is what is needed.

5. It is important to remember that LD students may take up to ten times longer to learn and will tire quickly. They have to try harder, which can be exhausting. Be aware that the pace of the normal class is likely to be too fast because they often need more time to process language. Make a conscious effort not to speak too quickly.

6. Make sure that the student feels safe and secure in your classroom and in your presence. Remember that all students, including LD students, have good days and bad days. Performance inconsistency is part of the problem, and it results in a great deal of the frustration felt by the LD student.

7. Be prepared to learn from the parents. Interest, involve and work closely with them. You need each other's help. Frequent contact should occur, once a day, once a week, or once a month depending on need. Use whatever works – home/school agendas, face-to-face meetings, phone calls or e-mails.

8. Ensure that information concerning the student is passed on when the student is in transition from one teacher to another, from one year to another, from one school to another, and from one country to another. Do not assume that this will be done automatically.

9. Keep your education ongoing. Get support for yourself. Draw on colleagues' expertise. Do not be afraid to acknowledge what you don't know.

Suggested strategies

1. Encourage pupils to be aware of and to evaluate the strategies they used to study and to learn. Study skills, like note taking and time organisation, need to be actively taught.

2. LD students need a lot of structure. Lists of the day's routines and expected behaviour can be of great help. Give plenty of warning when changes are made to the timetable, teacher or task.

3. LD students might have difficulty with such organisational tasks as keeping their things tidy at school, getting dressed, remembering their

PE kit, looking for something they have lost, packing their school bag, and organising the equipment needed for homework. The teacher should work with the student and the parents to devise strategies to help with organisation, such as lists, timetables, and colour-coded books.

4. LD students often need to be taught how to ask questions. All students, especially ones with LD, need to feel comfortable seeking assistance.

5. Break down learning into small, sequential tasks. Give specific examples.

6. Use lots of visual aids, such as overhead projectors, films, videos, slides, chalkboards, computer graphics, diagrams, charts, highlighting, under-lining, arrows and pictures to illustrate all subjects, including the teaching of language.

7. Repeat, repeat, repeat – both old and new materials, in different ways.

8. Provide the amount of structure and support that the student needs, not the amount of support and structure traditional for that grade or that classroom or subject.

9. Don't expect the student to listen and do simultaneously. For example, note taking can be extremely difficult for some.

10. Mark positively – tick the good bits. Mark for content – not presentation.

11. Allow the use of any learning tool necessary, such as tape recorders, spell checkers, misspellers dictionaries, laptops, voice-activated soft-ware, text readers and calculators. Teach keyboard and word-processing skills beginning in the primary school.

12. At all times avoid the use of sarcasm, continual and negative criticism, or bringing attention to the students' different needs in front of their peers. Recognise that these students will respond significantly better when encouraged, and when positive achievements are noticed and mentioned.

13. Playtime should not be used to complete work.

14. Catch the student being good and reward this behaviour.

15. Most importantly, seek opportunities to praise and build self-esteem.

This is a project of the Educational Support Committee of
The Federation of American Women's Clubs Overseas.
http://www.fawco.org. All rights reserved.

Authors' comments

There are considerable resource materials listed on the web site including Internet sites, as space did not allow us to list the resource materials in this book.

Programme delivery for ADHD students

An excellent resource for the teaching of children diagnosed with ADHD is: *All about ADHD The Complete Practical Guide for Classroom teachers,* by

Linda J Pfiffner, PhD. This book is indeed a practical guide for teachers and a useful checklist has been included below (Pfiffner 1996, p 149):

How to have an effective programme

1. Don't argue back.
2. Don't give unnecessary explanations.
3. Don't yell.
4. Don't take good behaviour for granted.
5. Don't follow negative rewards with a negative comment.
6. Don't give half-hearted praise in a tone suggesting you don't mean it.
7. Don't criticise or humiliate the student in front of the class.
8. Don't give in and let the student have the reward before he or she earned it.
9. Don't give in and let the student have the reward when they plead or throw tantrums.
10. Don't give too many second chances.
11. Don't forget about the programme or forget to complete the daily report card.
12. Don't expect too much or set the standards for reward too high for an individual ADHD student.
13. Don't expect too little.
14. Don't give up when the student loses interest in the reward.

Miller & Castellanos (1998, p376) have written effective goals of treatment for children with ADHD:

Goals of treatment

- Establish the collaborative treatment concept (child, parents, physician, school, other professionals.
- Educate the child, family, and school about the child's manifestation of AD/HD and related problems.
- Consider behavioural, emotional, academic, and medical issues (BEAM).
- Recognise the ecological factors (home, school, peers, community).
- Prioritize problems (primary or related) for management.
- Target achievable goals and set reasonable expectations.
- Address child's concerns and incorporate his or her suggestions.
- Increase structure and positive feedback.
- Emphasise problem ownership and personal responsibility.
- Cultivate a chronic condition management perspective.

- Prevent secondary academic, emotional, and social complications.
- Instill a sense of competence and hope in the child and family.

It is recommended that an IEP for a child with ADHD, incorporating and expanding the above goals of treatment, would help all concerned with the child. It is wise to include the child in the IEP writing. Miller and Castellanos (1998) write that the following are the most important points to consider for children with ADHD:

- Careful, comprehensive evaluation is crucial for appropriate management and follow-up of children and adolescents who have attention deficit/hyperactivity disorders.
- Medication can be highly effective as one component of a multimodal treatment plan.
- A team approach that incorporates the child as a key member is essential because self-management is the goal.

Activity-based reward programme

Many children who have been diagnosed as having ADD or ADHD may benefit from an activity-based reward programme. This is an individual programme using activities and privileges as rewards. Since ADD and ADHD students require immediate rewards, it is essential that the programme and rewards be organised before the plan is implemented.

Below is a programme taken from Linda J Pfiffner's book (Pfiffner 1996 p87):

1. What is the behaviour I am concerned about? Be specific.
2. How often does it happen? (The baseline).
3. What do I want the student to be doing instead? (The target behaviour).
4. How many times, or for how long must the student do the target behaviour to earn a reward?
5. What activity or privilege can be used as a reward? (Get input from the student).
6. When will the reward be given? (Remember immediate feedback is most effective).

It is a useful exercise to ask teachers to analyse their student's behaviour and to develop a programme using these questions to provide a structure. It is also useful to have all the teachers who are involved with teaching the ADHD child sit together to plan specific behaviours to be targeted so as to be consistent in treating the behaviour during the day. It is also more effective if you involve the student in the target behaviour and how it is to be treated. Ask the student to list the rewards if the behaviour improves.

The Concentration Cockpit: Explaining Attention Deficits To Children, developed by Dr Melvin D Levine, MD (Levine, 1988) is excellent for the regular classroom environment at the elementary level (see Appendix E: *Resources* for full details). The Concentration Cockpit 'is designed as an aid in the management of children with attention deficits. It is intended to serve as a means of clarifying the various symptoms of this deficit so that they can be more fully understood by the children, their parents, and their teachers'. The Cockpit consists of a large poster, which shows eight controls within an imagined cockpit. These controls are labelled as:

- mood (not getting much too sad or much too happy at the wrong times);
- behavioural (thinking before you do things);
- motor/verbal (not wasting movement and talking);
- social control (tuning out other kids when you need to);
- memory (remembering important things);
- appetite (not always wanting things and looking ahead);
- free flight (not daydreaming);
- sensory filtration (not paying attention to unimportant sounds and sights).

These controls are placed around a 'Master Control', which features four master controls:

- consistency (keeping up good work);
- tempo (not doing things so fast);
- motivation input (doing things that aren't exciting);
- arousal (staying awake while working or listening).

Authors' comments

Excellent results have been obtained using this method in a classroom where there are one or more ADHD children. The teacher explained the Concentration Cockpit from the poster to the entire class and handed out copies of the cockpit in reduced form to all students. The students were asked to rate themselves putting arrows in each of the controls from 0 meaning that they had a very big problem, 1 meaning a pretty big problem, 2 meaning a little problem, or 3 meaning no problem.

The teacher discussed the ratings in private with each individual student as a means of helping the student realise where there might be a problem and how the teacher would help the student to improve his/her control behaviour. The teacher also had a student/parent-teacher conference to explain the controls, and with those ADHD students, the parents were given copies of their child's Concentration Cockpit to use at home with their child. This is only one way to utilise the Concentration Cockpit. We have also observed the Cockpit being used in the LRC with individual children.

Technologies and the Special Needs student

AAA Math

This internet site contains:

- hundreds of pages of basic maths skills;
- interactive practice on every page;

- an explanation of the maths topic on each page;
- several challenge games on every page;
- randomly created maths problems.

The grade levels range from Kindergarten to 8th grade and the maths topics are extensive. An AAA Math CD is also available at < http://www.aaamath.com/>

Distance education

The Center for Talented Youth (CTY) at the Johns Hopkins University, Baltimore, Maryland provides academically-challenging courses in writing, mathematics, computer science, and physics, guided by CTY tutors. Distance Education uses online and CD formats to enable students to take accelerated courses year-round at home or school. Participants in the programmes must first be identified and qualified by the center's 'international talent search' (see Chapter 6, *Programme delivery and accountability*). These programmes are excellent. (More can be learned about the programmes by logging onto the CTY site at: <http://jhu/gifted.edu> e-mail: ctyinfo@jhu.edu).

Authors' comments

The CTY Distance Education writing programme, for example, matches a real author to the student and the two communicate through various writing assignments. One international school talented writer (Laura) was encouraged to enter the Talent Search (see Appendix D, *Case studies*) and qualified but did not take the CTY distance writing programme. Instead she attended a creative writing class at her local university.

Learning disabilities

The British Education Communications Technology agency (BECTA) <http://www.becta.org.uk> is an excellent site for technologies and learning disabilities. David Wilson (see below) has extensive experience with technologies and learning disabilities. For specific questions about technologies and learning disabilities it is advised to contact him at his co-ordinates at the end of his question and answer section (David Wilson, 2003).

David Wilson answers the question, 'What programmes can you recommend from personal experience as teaching aids for dyslexia and related specific learning difficulties for ages 5 to 15?'

'I strongly believe that you should start with a definition of the problem you are trying to solve. Are you trying to address dyslexia as a breakdown in the acquisition of basic skills? Are you trying to assist the student in accessing the subject-based curriculum? What does the Individual Education Plan/Educational Psychologist consider is the student's paramount needs?

What software is the student already being exposed to? What software does the school have? Start with a decent word processing package (one which you would use yourself, not a single-issue Special Educational

Needs-specific word processor with limited facilities). If you buy every SEN package in sight, you won't have time to familiarise yourself with them. Go for depth, not breadth, and do explore the Internet, if only to gather advice from colleagues (*eg* SENCO-Forum, Inclusive Education Forum).

I spent a long time speaking one-to-one with a representative from the British Dyslexia Association at the BETT national educational computing exhibition. We both agreed that compiling a list of 'prescribed software' is an inappropriate exercise. It's what you do with the software that matters; how it fits in with your non-ICT work; and how much the dyslexic child feels ownership of the learning process. Ask yourself what concrete problems the child has. The need to match sounds with words may suggest you use *Units of Sound*; spelling problems may be eased with *Starspell*; but the ICT should be only one weapon in your general armoury. It is no panacea. Get a stand-alone machine to trial and pilot new materials. Watch how the child reacts. Be prepared to dump a programme if it doesn't work. Just because the next-door school uses it doesn't mean it's good for you and your students.

You may have noticed messages about Integrated Learning Systems, which not only provide drill and practice but also record-keep. They are very expensive and the jury is still out about their effectiveness. What seems clear, however, is that you hand over complete responsibility for learning to a computer at your peril. You must know what the computer is doing and make sure that what it offers is precisely what you, the child, the parent and other teachers deem appropriate. Remember, most content-based software is good for revision, but poor at introducing new concepts. The latter is your, and your colleagues' job.

David Wilson

Learning Support Teacher
Equal Opportunities Department, Harton School,
Lisle Road, South Shields, NE34 6DL, UK
Email: DavidRitchieWilson@compuserve.com
Website: <http://www.tomwilson.com/david>

SuccessMaker

SuccessMaker provides individualised instruction to all students, including special needs students, enrolled in the programme. A further use of this excellent computer programme is individualising mathematics and some aspects of language arts for all students in a particular classroom or within a self-contained learning resource centre. This is a programme has had much success at international schools. SuccessMaker Enterprise is a K-12 service, which can be bought for computers or can be used on-line as a distance-learning programme for language arts and mathematics. The programme tests the student in specific areas and places the student at the levels at which the student will start to learn. The instruction is neither too easy nor too difficult but is at the right level for each individual student as identified by the initial testing. Here are some of the benefits and management systems that SuccessMaker advertises:

Benefits

- Progress reports show overall course performance for a student or group of students, allowing for timely interventions and course adjustments.

- Identification of skill areas in which a student is having difficulty drives individualised instructional decisions by teachers.

- IPM (Initial Placement Motion) automatically locates the student's starting level and presents appropriate instruction.

- Dynamic ordering finds the optimal sequence of instruction for each student.

- Continuous progress assessment adapts the course to the student's level, creating a successful learning experience and supporting steady growth.

- Tutorial intervention employs a variety of instructional strategies when students have difficulty.

- Retention check automatically activates at intervals during the learning process to ensure retention of previously presented skill.

Results Manager management system

This system provides data on-demand for teachers to monitor student progress. The reports show:

- overall performance in a course;

- skill objectives in which a student is having difficulty;

- global overview of group progress;

- forecast of time needed by individual students to reach instructional goals.

The Results Manager provides ongoing evaluation in the areas of reading, writing, mathematics, and thinking skills.

The authors have observed SuccessMaker in action at an international school for the elementary grades. Students spent about 20 minutes per day at the computer being instructed in mathematics. The individual student printouts were extensive and gave the teacher a lot of information in order to re-teach, or to extend teaching in certain areas where groups of students found the tasks too difficult. Students, who were able to progress at their own pace of learning, found the programme a positive experience, especially for those who were exceptionally talented in mathematics. (Full information can be found at <http://www.successmaker.com>).

Authors' comments

The original research on SuccessMaker on mathematics showed students' average performance for mathematics in England, with the use of SuccessMaker during nine months of school, increased their performance for mathematics by over one year. However, the programme is only as good as the teacher can direct it and is not recommended as a replacement to the teacher instructing the students but as a supplement (please see David Willson's comments in the learning disabilities section on technologies).

textHELP!

textHELP! Systems Ltd has created a portfolio of products for developing basic skills in reading, writing and comprehension. The software has been specifically designed for students with learning difficulties such as dyslexia who either have English as their native language or are learning English as a foreign language. textHELP! provides the tools which enable users to progress independently, gaining motivation and satisfaction in mainstream education, on mainstream computer programs promoting true inclusive education. This software has been used successfully in international schools with dyslexic students. (A demo copy of the programs can be obtained from E-mail: info@texthelp.com otherwise access the website at <http://www.texthelp.com>).

User's comment

'Due to my position as chair of the Educational Support Committee for the Federation of American Women's Clubs Overseas, I was given a copy of the textHELP programme to evaluate. For three years I have been using this program with a secondary international school student with significant LD problems. This student has found the program user-friendly and fun to use, and the quality of written work produced has improved dramatically. I can also see many potentials for using this program with ESL students.'

(Susan van Alsenoy, Chair FAWCO ESC)

The Learning Toolbox

The Learning Toolbox website is designed to assist secondary students with learning disabilities and ADHD to become more effective learners using research-based strategies. The Learning Toolbox is designed for independent use by students, special and general education teachers, and parents. <http://coe.jmu.edu/Learningtoolbox/>.

Authors' comments

This is an excellent website which is being used by many international schools and schools in the United States. It is user-friendly and is based on proven strategies.

Training of cognitive strategies

'In this program coloured cards and stencils are to be placed on one another so as to reproduce a model. All but one of the stencils are symmetric. In the asymmetric stencil a triangle is cut out. This stencil can be turned through 90 degrees thus making the task of reproduction a greater challenge. The models are presented on nine levels of difficulty. On the first level only one card and one stencil are needed to reproduce the model. On the ninth level up to nine stencils are superimposed. Even adults can have great difficulty reproducing these models correctly. This broad range of difficulties is a strong point of this program.

The final product – the correct or incorrect answer – is not as important as the path chosen by the trainee to find the solution. To understand the thought processes all activities of the trainee and the reactions of the programme are saved in a protocol. The program recognises 44 types of errors.' A demo can be seen at: <http://pedcurmac13.unifr.ch/CogStrat.html> (17 June 2002). A second program, Inductive Thinking, which can also be seen on this website, is excellent to use with students when they have completed the first program. Both programs can be ordered from the website.

The Cognitive Strategies program is recommended for all types of students, especially those who have strong visual reasoning skills or very weak visual reasoning skills. It is colourful and fun plus a learning tool for visual memory as well.

User's comment

'Cogstrat is a game where you are given 12 pieces of different colours and shapes. Above these you are given a pattern of using a number of these pieces. With the pieces given you must try to duplicate this shape. I liked the way that to pass the first five or so levels you just need to find a strategy and that as soon as you caught it the program got very entertaining. Then in the last levels (six-nine) it gives you patterns, which are harder to look through requiring you to think and to use your brain in another way than you are used to. The colours of the pieces were also very clear which made it easier to see the way the forms connected.

Overall the game was a great sensation except for a few of things that could easily be changed. When I first looked at the game I did not find a packet of information explaining how to play and what the goal of the game was. The lady's voice in the game was good at the beginning but after an hour or so it got very monotonous and started to annoy me. I found that this game was very well thought out and I recommend it to other people.'

(Cyrille Derché, 10th grade student, 1.4.2003)

Accountability

It cannot be emphasised enough that LRC support teachers be held accountable for the students in their charge by insisting that IEPs be written, progress reports frequently written for regular teachers and parents, portfolios be created, and testing up-dated. These also help parents and staff to understand the teaching process and to see what areas are being supported. The IEP forms the basis for lesson plans and can be used to show progress and be evaluated as to the efficacy of the programme. It is suggested that LRC support teachers keep a folder of work and a diary form of daily progress with their students. The school head should be made aware of the name of every student for whom IEPs have been created and frequently review their IEPs. Some checklists have been included below in order to help clarify the needs of students in the programme.

Chapter Seven

The role of the school to parents

How do we develop a positive working relationship with parents?

"The school is as important to me as it is to my child. I feel happy here with people who accept my child for who she is."

(Parent of a child with Special Needs).

In the international school system, the school plays an extremely important role in the life of the family. Very often, the school is the only social contact the family has in the new country and when the family has a child with special learning needs, the school becomes an extremely important part of the family's life. However, meeting the needs of the parents can often be as challenging as meeting the needs of the students as there are many emotions that govern their behaviour. These emotions may be demonstrated in aggressive behaviour that may alienate the school staff and may ultimately impact on the children. To try to help the parents, it is important to understand some of the 'seven deadly emotions' that might be experienced.

1. Blame

Parents may blame themselves for their child's learning difficulty. They may have a difficulty seeing it in their child and want to overcompensate. They may also blame the school for causing the child's learning difficulty, resulting in aggression towards the school. If their child has been identified as gifted but is under-achieving, the parents might blame the school for not attending to his/her learning needs rather than look at other reasons for the under-achievement.

2. Guilt

"If we had been in a different country, then this would never have happened/been allowed to progress so far/would have been dealt with better". The international life is one which very often does not take into account children's educational needs, and parents have little or no choice in the school their child attends. "If promotion equals a 'hardship' posting for a while, will this really affect my child's education?" Years later, they may feel it did.

3. Anger

Very often, some members of the family do not want to be in a particular country, away from 'home'. This obviously creates a negative attitude. Should the family have a child who needs extra support, they may feel angry at being in a place that may not supply the extra support the child needs and feel frustrated that they have to stay there to retain an income. In those schools where extra fees apply parents may also express anger to the school at the unfairness of having to pay extra for their child's LRC lessons.

4. Embarrassment

Parents want their children to 'fit in'. Any child who requires extra support to help develop their potential may feel that they are different and feel embarrassed. The Parent Evening when parents are told that their child needs support, or when parents complain that they are not being challenged enough, can be a nightmare, as some teachers may not always be tactful. Some parents of gifted children are reluctant to speak out at parent evenings even if they have a valid complaint as they may have overheard some parents of children with learning problems speaking with each other about how the gifted will get by with no extra accommodations and the school should concentrate special education funds on those with LD.

5. Threatened

Parents may feel threatened by teachers who may in turn feel threatened by parents. If parents feel that their child is not receiving the support services that are needed to reach his/her potential then they might appear to be very threatening towards teachers. If the child has exceptional ability, teachers may feel that they need to challenge the parents to prove that ability. This sets up difficult relations between the two bodies when both have the best interests of the child at heart. A high school teacher was overheard to say to one of her students, "If you are so intelligent, why is it that you have such poor grades?"

6. Incompetence

Teachers may feel that they are unable to cope with children of very high ability or with very specific learning needs, and if they are feeling insecure they may begin to doubt their own professional competence. This may make the teacher defensive or unwilling to adapt their programme as they feel they do not have the professional qualifications to do this.

7 Aggression

This is very often expressed by parents in international schools and can be very daunting when the teacher or school is verbally attacked. It is often a result of frustration. It is worth trying to put yourself in the situation of the parent – this may help to explain some of the comments that may come your way.

So how do we help parents?

Tell them!

Explain the difficulties that the child is having and how these can be supported in school. Parents are interested in knowing about their children's needs, eg what does it mean to be dyslexic? Why does it happen? What effects does it have?

Involve them!

The most frustrating thing for a parent is to be treated as if they know nothing about their own child. Certainly, the school has the educational expertise, but must include parents in the analysis of their child's difficulties and/or abilities. How are these manifested at home? When did the parent think that the child might be having problems or be tested for high abilities?

The answers to these questions may also give the teacher insight as a professional into the child's learning needs.

Inform them!

Very often once a parent understands the problem, they can work with the school to develop the child's learning potential at home. It makes life so much easier for you as a professional if you have the parents working with you as part of a teaching team. It is also more satisfying for you if you can share the successes and failures with another interested party ... and who could be more interested than a parent?

How do I do it?

Provide lunchtime/evening information sessions

Invite a speaker to talk to the parents about learning difficulties and the gifted/talented. Not only will this give you an educated body of parents, it will provide a forum for parents to discuss common concerns and mutual support. If you provide food and drink, or ask parents to bring their own lunch, this makes the meeting less formal and more conducive to 'chatting'.

Organise lunches or coffee sessions

These may come after the lunchtime sessions, once initial contacts have been made. Any social occasion where parents can get together to talk about their children, is helpful. Some parents may like to start an informal or formal support group for Special Needs children.

Supply information

Ask the Parent Association of the school to donate money to provide reading materials for parents of children with Special Needs. These can be kept in the school library and can be circulated in the same way as other books. In this way, parents are also using the school as a resource and become part of the 'community of learners'.

Involve them in the planning of the Individual Education Plan (IEP) for their child

This is crucial.

Invite them to stand for election to the Board

Parents need to be part of the organisation of a school and parents of Special Needs children also need to have input. By inviting parents to be part of the Board, they become instrumental in formulating policies and in helping to foster an understanding of the nature of Special Needs children. Since 20-50% of the school population requires some type of special support (excluding ESL) at some time, it is essential that their needs be represented at the highest level. Similarly, when parents have complaints or requests, these are often communicated to the Board, and it is helpful if a Board member has some specific expertise in this area.

Resources for parents

There are some excellent resources available for parents and the more the parents are informed and can be a constructive part of the teaching team, the easier it is for the Learning Resource teacher to do his/her job.

Schwab Learning is a programme from the Charles and Helen Schwab Foundation dedicated to helping children with learning differences be successful in learning and life. It provides parents with the information and support they need to help their children with learning difficulties. The information is easy to understand and is practical. As they state in their leaflet, *A Guide to Differences and Disabilities in Learning*, 'the more you know about how children learn, the more you can help your child.' (Charles and Helen Schwab Foundation 2001). The SchwabLearning website <http://www.schwablearning.org> has information on publications and details of services.

The Schwab guide has an excellent checklist (quoted below) for parents outlining what to look for at different stages of their child's development. By using this parents can identify if their child has certain needs and will also be prepared for working with the teacher.

Preschool

❐ Speaks later than most children.

❐ Problems saying speech sounds.

❐ Slow vocabulary growth; often unable to find the right word.

❐ Difficulty rhyming words.

❐ Trouble learning numbers, letters, days of the week, colours, shapes.

❐ Extremely restless and easily distracted.

❐ Problems interacting with peers.

❐ Difficulty following directions or routines.

❐ Fine motor skill delays.

Grades K-4

❐ Slow to learn connections between letters and sounds.

❐ Consistent reading and spelling errors, word reversals (was/saw), letter reversals (b/d), inversions (m/w), transpositions (left/felt) and substitutions (there/then).

❐ Transposes number sequences and confuses arithmetic signs (+, -, x, /, =).

❐ Trouble remembering facts.

❐ Slow to learn new skills; relies heavily on memorisation.

❐ Impulsive; has difficulty planning.

❐ Difficulty making and keeping friends.

❐ Unstable or unusual pencil grip.

❐ Trouble remembering sequences and telling time.

❐ Poor coordination; unaware of physical surroundings, accident-prone.

Grades 5-8

☐ Slow to learn prefixes, suffixes, root words, and other reading strategies

☐ Spells incorrectly, frequently spells the same word differently in a single piece of writing.

☐ Avoids reading aloud.

☐ Difficulty with word problems in math.

☐ Trouble with handwriting.

☐ Avoids writing compositions.

☐ Poor recall of facts.

☐ Problems with sequenced actions – taking turns, playing team sports.

☐ Problems understanding body language, facial expressions and personal space.

High school and young adults

☐ Continues to have problems spelling incorrectly.

☐ Avoids reading and writing.

☐ Trouble taking tests.

☐ Weak memory skills.

☐ Difficulty adjusting to new setting; making transitions.

☐ Works slowly.

☐ Inability to form positive peer relationships.

☐ Pays too little attention to details or focuses on them too much.

☐ Misreads information.

☐ Difficulty summarising, generalising and grasping concepts.

By using this type of checklist the parents can identify that their own child has certain needs and is already prepared to work with the teacher. We suggest that you look at the Schwab website for further publications and details of their services.

Another useful resource is *The Parent's Guide to Learning Disabilities*, a user-friendly guide for parents to help their children with specific difficulties – ranging from not completing homework to having a short attention span. There are several examples because, as the authors say, 'Parents are likely to be more successful implementing those interventions they think are best for themselves and their child rather than attempting to implement interventions suggested by a third party who would not have the same insight the parents have relative to their child's behaviour' (McCarney and Bauer 1991, p5).

Dr Mel Levine, founder of the non-profit institute for the understanding of differences in learning, All Kinds of Minds, manages a useful website at <http://www.allkindsofminds.org> (28 April 2002). The organisation will help in the creation of a learning profile, which pinpoints a child's strengths and weaknesses in learning. 'Once this profile is created, All Kinds of Minds provides the language and tools for parents, educators and clinicians to develop a concrete, practical action plan to help a child succeed.' Dr Levine's most recent book, *A Mind at a Time*, is currently on *The New York Times Best Seller List* (April 22, 2002).

Authors' comments

Parents might be interested in reading this book, *Effective Learning Support in International Schools,* in order to be more informed about the subject of special learning needs of students.

Chapter Eight

Evaluation and appraisal of programmes and personnel
How do you know if it has been done?

"With all these tools, there must be something I can evaluate."

Seven key stages for the evaluation of a Learning Resource Centre (LRC) should be considered:

- the assessment and identification process;
- up-to-date and appropriate resource materials;
- effectiveness of the instruction through IEP achievement;
- investigating process for challenging and motivating students;
- effectiveness of matching and fine-tuning instruction;
- ongoing monitoring, documenting each step;
- evaluating LRC personnel.

Formal and informal evaluation of the programme and personnel is essential. The head of school should define the job description and the evaluation process at the hiring phase and there should be written evaluation policies for the LRC staff. It is recommended that the entire international school staff be involved in the evaluation process of the LRC's programme and that forms be presented to the staff to complete about the effectiveness of the unit.

Formal evaluation of LRC personnel

As in all schools and departments, the programme is only as good as the people who implement it. In order to ensure that the programme meets its goals and is staffed by effective teachers, on-going appraisal is necessary. Whereas we acknowledge that it is extremely important for schools to provide on-site training for student teachers and trainee psychologists, it is essential that these personnel are strictly supervised. Using trainee psychologists to administer in-depth tests, such as the Wechsler scales is forbidden (Wechsler 1991 p10).

Evaluate! Evaluate! Evaluate! Document! Document! Document!

1. Have a clear job description that is explicit in all areas. If a specialist in testing is required, ask for one! If schools want a teacher who can be flexible and supportive, they need to ask for one! Very often administrators just put basic qualifications down on a job description or leave out key specialist qualifications and then the number of applications from non-specialists disappoints them.

2. Interview in person! It is not always possible but interviews over the phone are just not the same. Walk round the school with the candidates and notice how they interact with children. This is crucial. Ask 'what if' type questions. Try to find out if the candidate is well balanced and emotionally stable. This is a tricky one but crucial if the teacher is to do their job properly … especially in an international school where the teachers might themselves be suffering from culture shock. Can they cope with living in a foreign country? With teaching 'difficult' children? Do they have ulterior motives for teaching Special Needs children? Do they themselves need to be needed? This all may sound very cynical, but it is certainly worth thinking about. After all, the goal is to help the children and not have the school used as an emotional 'prop'. On pages 56 you will find job descriptions for hiring an Educational Psychologist and sample questions of how an interview should reflect the LRC's philosophy and practices.

3. Evaluate! Make the teachers responsible for their teaching. Do you expect results? Are they able to achieve them? Is the programme appropriate for the child? Are the parents involved? Does the classroom teacher support the goals? Is there collaboration between the Special Needs teacher and the classroom teacher? Do they 'get on'? Go back to the job description and use it as a basis for the evaluation. Ask the teacher to set term goals and then be evaluated on them. Emphasise the documentation of all important issues occurring between staff, parents-staff, staff-students because, down the road, a document could clarify a situation which might come up.

4. Provide Professional Development! Encourage the teachers to take advantage of any professional development that is available. Ask them to provide professional development for parents, teachers and administrators!

Curriculum

1. What term goals have you set?
2. What goals have you set for the children in your care?
3. What goals have you set for the year?
4. How do these goals fit into the LRC curriculum and your IEPs?
5. How do these goals fit with the overall development plans/goals of the school?

Professional development

The following were questions a school head asked the LRC staff in order to help the professional development process:

1. What/when was your last in-service experience? And how did you use that experience in your teaching?
2. What in-service/professional development experience would enhance your teaching and refresh you?
3. What is your long-term professional development plan: what are your needs? Where do you see yourself headed professionally? How can the school help you to reach your goals?
4. What would you like to try that is new this week, month, term, or year *eg* a project, a unit, a method, an approach? Write up a proposal – describe it, when you will be doing it and how it can be assessed.
5. What are your strengths?
6. What are your weaknesses?
7. What can you do to enhance your strengths and strengthen your weaknesses?
8. What can the school do to support you in this?

Other matters to be raised

1. Would you like to take a day off to visit another school?
2. Please be prepared to tell me about any of your students I choose to ask you about.
3. What other areas of evaluation do you think might help us during the evaluation conference?

It is important for the LRC to be transparent, flexible and proud to show the head/appraiser the 'inner workings'. If the head does not readily enter the LRC to assess and evaluate, invite him/her to join the LRC for a day and ask him/her to evaluate the programme and LRC staff. Heads have so much to do that they seem to leave the LRC to function without regular visits. But it is important that the LRC is valued by the head as any other section of the school and therefore similarly evaluated. In addition, heads are often confronted by parents demanding specific services for their child. If the head has a comprehensive knowledge of the LRC these discussions with parents go much more smoothly.

The following Assessment/Evaluation/Reporting form was downloaded from: <http://www.manning.k12.ia.us/performanceassessment/aerhand-out.html>

Assessment/Evaluation/Reporting			
We use to...	But...	So now...	Because...
Place more emphasis on what students could not or should not do	we learned that this focus undermined the confidence of many students and that we could be more supportive of their accomplishments	we begin with what students can do, then consider their learning needs	this helps them to develop confidence and gives a foundation for building and further refining skills and knowledge
fail students who did not meet preset expectations for behaviours or ability to do tasks	we found that some students doubted their ability to learn and this increased the probability of their dropping out of school	teachers give students the support to allow them to make continuous progress	this maintains their self-esteem and confidence, thus prompting further learning by strengthening the disposition to learn
use pencil/paper tasks as the main way of assessing and evaluating students	we now know that this gave a limited view of what students could do	we encourage students to represent their learning in a variety of ways (show what they know)	this provides opportunities for more students to demonstrate their intelligence and to be successful learners
Compare learners to each other	this made comparisons more important than the actual learning	each learner is evaluated on what he or she can do in relation to expectations and skills that are widely held as being important, continually refined, and purposefully applied	this helps each student feel valued as a learner and builds on individual strengths, which encourages a good start toward lifelong learning
use checklists for students' report cards	they gave limited information about what students could do	we use information from observations, conferences, and collections of students' work to develop anecdotal reports	they give more comprehensive information about what students can do
use letter grades for reporting students' progress (A, B, C) (G, S, NI)	letter grades were dependent on teacher and parent interpretation and often focused on surface knowledge rather than understanding	we use anecdotal reports to describe students' learning	they give a more detailed picture of what students can do and identify future learning goals
Exclude students from assessment and evaluation process	this did not encourage the development of self-evaluation skills	students encouraged to take a more active role in assessing and evaluating their own progress and, with the help of the teacher, set future learning goals	as students construct meaning of the world around them, this process encourages self-evaluation, independent learning, and a commitment to further learning
plan conferences for parents and teachers to exchange information	this often overlooked the people with the most relevant information – the students as developing learners	teachers are beginning to plan ways to include students in the conference with parents	together, they can develop a shared understanding of students' abilities, interest and learning needs, resulting in the setting of realistic learning goals

Taken from: Supporting Learning, Understanding and Assessing the Progress of Children in the Primary Program, Province of British Columbia, Ministry of Education, 1993. Permission granted for use in training.

The sample job descriptions for LRC staff in Chapter Four, *Organisation, services and personnel*, could very easily become the basis of formal staff evaluation and of the special needs/learning support programme. For example, rating scales from one to five could be written for each statement with one being excellent to five unsatisfactory. Thus, the head/senior administrator and LRC staff would be responsible in dual rating (head and each LRC member) as a means for a constructive dialogue. The evaluation of the LRC by the entire school staff (including the head of school), during or at the end of the school year (see below), can be very helpful. The Special Needs student interviews of how they see their instruction within the classroom and the LRC (overleaf) are another means of evaluating the LRC programme. The ECIS Special Needs/Learning Support accreditation guidelines could also be added to an evaluation packet.

Learning Support Centre

Evaluation For School Year (_____)

For within Learning Support Centre and/or Classroom Support
Thank you for completing these three questions and returning to the LRC by _____.

Name:

1. What has worked well this year?

2. What would you like to be improved?

3. What are your specific needs and suggestions for the LRC for the next school year?

Additional comments:

Student interviews

It is helpful to include the students' point of view regarding effective learning support at their schools. The Student Interviews form was created by the authors and distributed to various international schools. The form and results of the student interviews follow.

Effective learning support

(Use other side of this paper, if necessary)

1. Student interviews

How has receiving learning support affected my life?

_____
_____
_____
_____

2. What has worked well for me in learning support?

_____
_____
_____
_____

3. What has not worked well for me in learning support?

_____
_____
_____

4. What has worked well for me in the regular classrooms?

_____
_____
_____

5. What has not worked well for me in the regular classrooms?

_____
_____
_____

6. Suggestions for improvement in my:

Regular classrooms

_____
_____
_____

Learning Support

_____
_____
_____

7. Any other comments?

_____

(Haldimann & Hollington, 2004)

Data from the student interview forms

1. I like getting help with my reading and writing. It helped me to learn to read and to like reading. It helped me learn new words. It helped me to know how to write essays. Made things easier, it's fun, it makes me more confident at my reading and writing. It is good for me, I got better in reading. It has been good for me and I have nearly caught up with the other children. Makes me smarter, I could read better and do a lot of stuff that I couldn't do before. It helps me do better work (write up, essay). I get better grades because I have a chance to see where I go wrong then do better in that subject area. It has affected my life in many ways because there are different learning styles that they teach us here and not in class.

2. Re-reading instructions in class. To explain things in a different way. Giving me time to figure it out. It helps me get more organised and because I get help with all kinds of English stuff. To go over assignments in LS. Reading and writing. The read naturally programme. It helps in small groups. The read naturally timing. It helps to be in small groups. My reading and spelling has gotten better, I've been more willing to learn. It's better coming out 1-1 with a teacher. Get some extra school time to work on major projects and essays. A lot of things. One is studying for tests. Asking questions on homework if I need it.

3. Using headphones for semiophonie. Math – not so good but improving. I am missing out but it's best to stick with support until ready.

4. Extra time, read questions for/with me, explain again, give me breaks in between projects, having a printed instruction sheet to follow, allow me to get up and move (I am ADD). I need to draw to concentrate, I can't just sit there doing nothing. Addition and math teacher works 1-1 with me sometimes (and for everybody), reading at right speed. Working alone or with one person. You can write a story and it does not matter if I do mistakes. PYP units of inquiry – straight forward. Different ways of projects – teacher makes it easier for me. I am more able to see what is going on and I get lots of help from teachers when I need or ask. A lot because teachers help me if I need help with something. Also if I don't understand a question they explain it to me.

5. I don't have time to think, I get distracted by the slightest thing. They do not give me enough time to think. Times tables test too quick. I am too shy to read in front of the class. Groups do not include me. I don't feel comfortable reading in the classroom. Groups don't let me write or read. The math, IT – poor typer – sometimes frustrated in regular classroom. Sometimes I find it hard to take in things because the teacher may work too fast for me but I ask and then it's usually OK. When students use these big long words, I don't understand them.

6. Explain stuff different ways, ask me to bring in my work/projects and check for me it is OK, work to my mom too, so she knows what I'm doing. Giving me more time to work, I work better when there are certain amount of people like two or three because I have problems and peo-

ple might make fun of me, helps me in organising my projects. I learn better when I have something to do (fiddle with), I work best with a small group like two, three, four, five because people make fun of me if I ask questions. Give more time to get answer to time-table test in class, less writing – my hand feels sore. That they respect me more with my reading and writing problems. In LS I would like more reading and write stories. They would respect that we are not so good at reading and spelling. More reading in LS. More time in LS, the opportunity to come here during my IB schedule. To have the teachers help me and show me how to study for my tests. In LS, more time with them because usually on Monday and Tuesday I have one class and on Wednesday I have a double lesson which works for me really well because I can get more work done and it helps me to study.

7. I go to Eagles Nest, a homework club after school. It helps me get my homework done before I go home, great! It's fun! It's embarrassing when I have to be pulled out of class by the learning support teacher when no one else has to go. I can get more work done and it helps me to study.

Postscript

Martha Haldimann's and Angela Hollington's *Effective Learning Support in International Schools* is at once a preserving and a progressive witness to what all good teachers and administrators know to be the secrets of outstanding education – intense focus on the strengths and weaknesses of an individual child, the positive affirmation of individual difference, and the adjustment of learning strategies and resources to meet the advancement of children rather than the mindless preservation of an educational bureaucracy.

With eloquent reference to educational theory and abundant introduction of practical classroom situations and 'how to' interventions, Haldimann and Hollington affirm what the French philosopher, Rousseau, wisely knew – children stand at the centrepoint of learning and the more we know about them and the more we adjust instructional strategies to their capacities, ultimately the more successful and fulfilling education is for student and teacher.

Haldimann and Hollington forward the Optimal Match model as a philosophy of education for international school educators. In so doing, they are acutely aware that they are confronting prevailing educational practice worldwide. Haldimann and Hollington insist that educators must respect the uniqueness and worth of human individuality or difference rather than disability, that educators recognise that all individuals differ and that when these differences are dealt with positively, students will be able to develop to their full potential and capitalise upon their own ability and styles.

Haldimann and Hollington strike at those many who worship 'a mist of sameness', and who are moved by the vision of large numbers of students learning basically the same thing, at the same time, and with the same degree of accomplishment. In this monolithic climate, intellectual and emotional differences are considered distasteful and are denied. Attention to individual difference is considered 'time-consuming' and 'distracting'.

Haldimann and Hollington provocatively counter in the name of quality education those notions entertained of educational theorists such as E D Hirsh that 'we need to reject the ill-founded notions that every child learns naturally at his or her own pace and that teaching the child is more important than teaching the subject'. Haldimann and Hollington value as a rational approach to education the delicate balance of child and subject matter directed by the teacher but informed by information from various sources. Additionally, *Effective Learning Support* builds on the distinctive strengths of international schools. Strikingly independent and accustomed to individual difference in language and culture, international schools – when fully realised – already possess the habits of mind and practice to achieve Optimal Match for their respective students. Naturally, certain limits have to be set on the full range of individual challenges that can be handled in any one school – simply from a personnel and resource standpoint – but in numerous cases, the possibility of an international school fulfilling well individual difference through disciplined means is greater than often originally conceived. Haldimann and Hollington persuasively help administrators and teachers realise these possibilities by drawing on the best theory and practice and matching these with existing accomplishments over the last few decades at selected international schools.

William G Durden, President, Dickinson College, Carlisle, Pennsylvania

Appendix A

Glossary of terms

AMA	American Medical Association
ACECY	Advisory Committee on Exceptional Children and Youth
ADD	Attention Deficit Disorder
ADHD	Attention Deficit Hyperactivity Disorder
CAS	Creative, Action, Service; component of the International Baccalaureate Diploma Program
CST	Classroom Support Teacher
CTY	Center for Talented Youth
DEA	Drug Enforcement Agency
DTLA	Detroit Tests of Learning Aptitude
ERB	Educational Records Bureau
ESL	English as a Second Language
FDA	Federal Drug Administration
GORT	Gray Oral Reading Tests
HMSO	Her Majesty's Stationery Office
IB	International Baccalaureate
IEP	Individual Educational Plan
IGCSE	International General Certificate Secondary Education
IQ	Intelligence Quotient
LRC	Learning Resource Centre
MYP	Middle Years Program of the International Baccalaureate
PPVT	Peabody Picture Vocabulary Test
PSAT	Preliminary Standardised Achievement Test
PTA	Parent Teacher Association
PTSD	Post Traumatic Stress Disorder
PYP	Primary Years Programme of the International Baccalaureate
SAT I	Standardised Achievement Test-I: Reasoning
SEN	Special Educational Needs
TEWL	Test of Early Written Language
TONI	Test of Nonverbal Intelligence
TOWL	Test of Written Language
TOWS	Test of Written Spelling
VMI	Visual Motor Integration
WDCK/JN	Woodcock Johnson
WISC	Wechsler Intelligence Scale for Children
WRAT	Wide Range Achievement Test

Appendix B

Workshops

It is important that parents and teachers are kept informed about special learning needs and this may be done by information sessions, regular updates in school literature, workshops or practical activities. The following information has been included as schools might find it useful in raising the awareness of Special Needs throughout the school. It is recommended that orientation at the beginning of the term include a section on special learning needs and regular time at staff meetings is given to discussing this issue.

Workshops

Optimal Match Presentation

Useful questions for discussion by schools that are introducing/practising the Optimal Match Programme

1 How do you try to ensure that the learning needs of all your students are appropriately addressed?

2 How do you try to ensure that students are being challenged at their appropriate level, and how do you know that you are meeting their needs?

3 In what areas do you feel in need of help in order to deliver your content areas to a wide range of abilities?

4 What can the staff do together to address the learning needs of all our students?

5 Do you have what you suspect are hidden gifts and talents of students in your classroom, and how do you propose dealing with them?

6 What other questions do you have concerning the learning needs of students in your classroom?

There are several ways to present these questions to your staff. You could hand out these questions and ask the staff to complete the questions in writing and given to the Optimal Match development committee or to the head of school. You could discuss these questions within a particular section of the school and present in writing your conclusions to the committee or head of school. You could also hand out the questions to the staff a few weeks before initiating an Optimal Match presentation and ask the staff to be prepared to participate in a discussion based upon the questions. If a member of your staff had attended the Optimal Match Network Institute (OMNI, see Appendix E, *Resources*), you could end the workshop with an oral report of the issues and recommendations presented at OMNI.

Learning Disabilities

Instructions for staff workshops

Goals:

- to develop an awareness of learning disabilities;
- to propose procedures for referral of students with learning disabilities;
- to discuss classroom accommodations for students with learning disabilities;
- to answer individual questions about learning disabilities;
- to evaluate effectiveness of workshop on teacher knowledge of learning disabilities.

1. The school's director should divide the staff into groups of five or six and give each member the *Accommodations Checklist* (see opposite) for group discussion (The checklist could be photocopied and placed upon the other side of these instructions.) The groups should contain staff members who teach in the same level of the school. The school's Special Needs staff should also be included in the groups as well as the school head.

2. Each group should designate a group leader who will lead the discussion and record decisions to be reported later to all staff attending the workshop.

3. The group leader should write down all comments the group would like to make about students with learning disabilities or issues regarding learning disabilities the group would like to be reported.

4. Discussions should centre upon how to meet specific learning needs of a selected student or students within the regular classroom.

5. The following points may be of help to the discussion:

   a. What type of accommodations could be utilized? See also the *Accommodations Checklist.*

   b. What type of alternatives for assessment and grading of this (these) students could be used in the class?

   c. Are IEPs (Individual Educational Plans) needed for these students in the regular classroom? Should regular classroom teachers be involved in the writing up of IEPs for these students, and should the students also be involved in this process?

   d. Do classroom teachers need extra support within the classroom for this (these) student(s)? And if so, for which subject(s)?

   e. Do these students need more tutoring, or one-on-one help by a resource teacher? And if so, who should be assigned to supervise these cases (the regular classroom teacher, Director, resource teacher)?

6. After the reporting session, all written comments should be collected and Accommodation Checklists collected for each student. The checklists

should be photocopied for each teacher who teaches these students and a copy placed in the LRC files and student file in the school office. The written comments should be compiled and each staff member receive a copy.

Accommodations checklist for students in the regular classroom

Student's Name: Grade: Date:

Accommodations   Acceptable
                                                (tick as appropriate)

Accommodation	
Alternative grading	❏
Peer tutoring	❏
Seat in front of class	❏
Abbreviated assignments	❏
Alternative materials	❏
Vocabulary sheets in advance	❏
Extended test time	❏
Test taking along (in another room)	❏
Taped tests	❏
Taped test answers	❏
Oral test	❏
Scribe (note-taker)	❏
Lecture notes in advance	❏
Taped textbooks	❏
Tape recorder in class	❏
Laptop in class	❏
Homework assignments monitored	❏
Homework assignments and projects in advance	❏
Assignments completed on computer/printout	❏
No writing required (tapes, projects, oral report, *etc*)	❏
IEP for regular classroom	❏
Glasses required	❏
Other	❏

Standardised testing

Some questions for a workshop on standardised testing

Here are some questions posed by staff members at an international school to stimulate a lively discussion about the pros and cons of standardised testing. You might notice that most of these questions address the stereotypical negative arguments, which were discussed earlier in the body of this book. Also, you can probably perceive the hostility in some of the teachers' questions. The discussion centres on the use of the Educational Records Bureau Comprehensive Testing Program IV (ERB) but could also apply to other group standardised tests. One idea as to how to use these questions would be to hand the questions out to the staff and ask them to pose other questions in writing. The Educational Psychologist and/or the Learning Resource Centre coordinator could then lead the discussion with plenty of ammunition from this book to support group standardised testing at international schools. This would also be the time to pass out copies of the Mills and Durden (1996) article on standardised testing at international schools for a second discussion.

1. What use are the ERBs to a developing world student or any student who is not American?

2. What use are the trivial questions found in the tests?

3. The ERBs are fact-based content, and how can this be of use in an international school whose content is skill based?

4. As the ERB tests do not match grade level curricula in an international school, why should they be administered as the choice of a standardised test?

5. How is standardised testing relevant to international schools?

6. What is the statistical significance of the number of cultural biased questions?

7. Is it possible for a non-US student to guess at the questions on an ERB grade level test and score at the National Public School norm or at the Suburban norm?

8. What use are the ERB tests to an international school, which is process-oriented rather than content oriented?

9. Why has ECIS endorsed the ERB tests over other group standardised tests from either the US or other English-speaking countries?

Simulations For Learning Disabilities

These simulations could be used to introduce a workshop on learning disabilities. Particularly important is for the staff and/or parents to get a feeling about what a learning disabled student might be experiencing daily. Simulations 2, 3, and 4 were created to give the participants the sense of frustration, anxiety, and tension of F.A.T. City which is a workshop developed by Richard D Lavoie (see Appendix E, *Resources*) can be found on a video by the same name. The simulations are designed to put the participants in the skin of LD students to better understand their feelings and suffering.

Simulation 1

- Hand out a blank piece of paper to each participant. State that "You might have seen children who have difficulties with fine-motor coordination, which shows up in their messy or sometimes unreadable handwriting. This exercise will give you a feeling of what it is like to have to combine visual perception, visual perception of the written word and numbers, and fine-motor control". Ask the participants to put their pencil/ pen in their non-writing hand. Then very rapidly say, "I would like you to write the following. You only have one minute to complete the task. I will be timing you (show the stopwatch and start it after saying) *"Fine motor co-ordination is very difficult when I write the numbers 8,3,5,2,69,17 with this hand"*. Then ask the participants to write down (on the back of the paper) the sensations they had while writing and trying to remember what to write.

  Ask the participants to volunteer to tell the group how they felt while doing the simulation after which state, "You have just experienced difficulties with some fine-motor coordination and maybe some memory problems and tension of being timed. You can see how difficult it might be for an LD child to combine all the skills needed for effective writing. And what if one of the difficulties is writing numbers correctly? Some LD children confuse 6 and 9, or 3, 5 and 2, or 1 and 7. Let us increase the cues given and try to write the sentence again, still with your non-writing hand and copying the same sentence from the overhead thus giving you a visual cue. Again, you will have one minute in which to complete the exercise".

  Ask them to write down their feelings and for volunteers to tell the others what they felt. State, "You probably see that a learning disabled student may need as many assorted cues as possible and enough time in which to complete the task. And, the timing aspect was used to show you that some LD students need more time in order to complete their work. This would be the same at home when they are doing their homework. In addition, the sentence in the exercise was spoken rapidly to help you realise that some of these students have memory and concentration problems. This means that they may not always remember all of what is necessary from orally presented instructions when they are required to write something. For example, if homework assignments were given out only orally, you can be sure that some LD students will not be able to remember all that is required. That is why it is important to provide visuals along with oral presentation of classwork and homework assignments. Some students may also have trouble taking notes and listening at the same time and might need a scribe. And, you can only imagine the problems ESL learning disabled students may be experiencing – a nightmare for them. Regarding allowing extended test taking time and giving more time for completing work in the classroom, a lot of research has been conducted with LD and regular students. The research results show that when everyone is given extended test time, regular students usually do not use it, but LD students do. This is why LD students with documented LD qualify for extended test time on SATs, IGCSEs, and IB tests, for example".

Simulation 2

- State, "Many students with learning disabilities have difficulty in processing printed information. You will be given a piece of paper face down which has some sentences written on the other side". Hand out the following and tell the participants to work with their neighbour and that they have only three minutes in order to figure out what is written on the page:

St ySi ati fW LD P ou Wight Se

or mul ouo hat a ers e

n."saidB y."W

"Comeo ets

r

ehav di cku i o n.W

eto pth sc

eqon' not

thavea her".

- Ask the staff to use the reverse of the fine-motor co-ordination paper again to record the sensations they had while trying to figure out the story. Ask for volunteers to describe their feelings. State "It is fairly easy to show what being learning disabled is all about by focusing on dyslexia. You see how jumbled up these letter and words may seem while a dyslexic student is trying to read, especially when they have the problem of reversing (b for d), inverting (u for n), or transposing letters and syllables. And another difficulty for them is that they might see the words or letters on two lines rather than on one straight line".

(Correct Title and Sentence: Story Simulation of What a LD Person Might See "Come on", said Betsy. "We have to pick up this corn. We don't have another.")

Simulation 3

- Hand out photocopies of the following face up (vocabulary words) in front of each staff member. Ask a participant to read the vocabulary words and ask if they all understand their meanings. Next ask the participants to turn over the vocabulary page and read the paragraph to their neighbour:

Side 1: Vocabulary words to study

are	graph	between
if	consists	isolated
continuously	known	corresponding
making	curve	only
draws	often	variation
with	one	table
points	values	relation
variables	set	

Side 2: Paragraph to read

"If the known relation between the variables consists of a table of corresponding values, the graph consists only of a set of isolated points. If the variables are known to vary continuously, one often draws a curve to show the variation."

(*Basic College Math*, Michael Michaelson, 1945)

- Again ask the participants to record their feelings and ask for a volunteer to describe his/her feelings.

- State "LD students may not be able to transfer isolated words they have learned to a paragraph about a subject they do not know. It is similar to the problem some LD students have with spelling words – they can learn the words for a spelling test and maybe get them all correct but are not able to use them out of that context in writing assignments". Point out that along with reading comprehension difficulties, LD children are not always able to recognise change of print and will be additionally confused.

Simulation 4

- Cut out and photocopy enough copies of the two pictures (overleaf) but only hand out the unfocused picture, face down, to the staff. State "In addition to seeing letters or words in the wrong directions, some LD students have difficulty bringing meaning to what they see. Their vision is fine but they cannot perceive it or bring meaning to it unless they are directly taught what it is. Because we can see something, it does not necessarily mean that some LD students are seeing the same thing. We might say to them – look at it harder or longer, or you are not trying hard enough – assuming that overcoming a learning problem is motivation. With this last simulation, I am sure you will be motivated to see what is in the picture". Tell the participants that they will have three minutes to try to figure out what is in the picture and write the answer down to the left of the picture. Tell them again that you will be timing them with the stopwatch. After three minutes tell the staff to stop and again write down their sensations they felt. Next, ask for at least five volunteers to tell the staff what they have seen in the picture. Do not indicate what the picture shows. Then place a transparency of the picture in an enlarged form and ask if this helps them to find the cow in the picture. If not, hand out smaller copies of the cow outline.

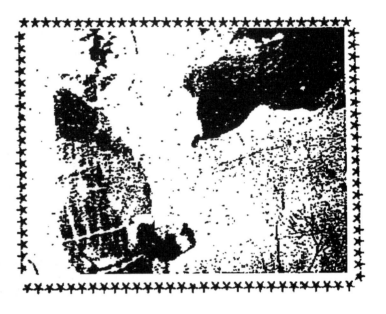

- State "Although you were trying very hard to see what was in the picture and were certainly motivated, some of you might have needed to have the example right in front of you as a prop in order to see what was in the picture".

Collect all materials explaining that you will make a summary of the experiences of what the participants had written, processes needed to execute the simulations, and you will give out summary copies to all the participants later for their reference. At this point, you might want to hand out the Smith Checklist of Characteristics of Learning Disabilities for the participants to complete about themselves as another way of summarising up the experience.

Authors' comments

The simulations could also be used at a workshop for parents to help them begin to understand how their child/children might be feeling all day long at school. Simulations 2,3,4 were taken from Richard Lavoie's F.A.T. City workshop video (see Appendix E, *Resources*). Mr Lavoie has kindly given permission to publish the simulations 2,3,4. The first simulation was created by Martha Haldimann.

Appendix C

Handouts

The following handouts, when appropriate, could be distributed during a consultation with parents after testing and/or used in a workshop situation.

The Qatari Centre for the Gifted and Talented
(Dr Taisir Subhi, ECHA National Correspondent, Jordan, 2001)

Why let them walk when they can fly?

Mission statement

To make education an enjoyable, exciting and worthwhile experience for gifted and talented children.

The Qatari Centre for the Gifted and Talented (QC/GT) assists children to achieve their full potential by raising awareness amongst as well as giving support to teachers, parents, educational policy makers, other professionals and the wider educational community.

The purpose of this article is to provide an explanation of the provisions for gifted and talented children in the State of Qatar. The article concerns itself with an overview of the State's experiences, practices, and current thinking on a number of major issues in the area of identification and the development of giftedness and creativity.

Gifted education in the State of Qatar has been promoted and the Ministry of Education and Higher Education has established the Qatari Centre for the Gifted and Talented (QC/GT). Scholars and interested people are planning to form a law to enforce consideration of gifted children in education. In addition, a national association for gifted will be formed.

Schooling in the State of Qatar is organised around three cycles: elementary (6-12 year olds), preparatory (13-15 year olds), and secondary (16-19 year olds). All schools follow the curriculum laid down by the Ministry of Education and Higher Education.

Gifted children are identified in this country as those who have demonstrated high ability (including high intelligence), high creativity, and high task commitment. In the adopted definition, standardised intelligence tests, creativity tests, and achievement tests measure abilities. Task commitment is measured by tests of achievement, rating scales, and judgment of teachers and parents.

The multiple criteria identification procedure adopted by the Qatari Centre for the Gifted and Talented, is based on a number of principles (or rationales), including:

- Gifted and talented children should be identified as early as possible in their educational careers;

- The focus of identification is not to label students, but to recognise and respond to gifted and talented students' educational needs;
- The identification of gifted and talented students requires the utilization of formal and informal measures obtained from many sources in a wide variety of settings;
- Identification instruments and procedures must match with the programme provided to gifted and talented children.

The Qatari Centre for the Gifted and Talented, a non-profit governmental institution, is a national centre for students, teachers, parents, educators, other professionals and community leaders who attempt to address the unique talents as well as those children who may be able to develop their talent's full potential with appropriated educational experiences. The QC/GT supports and develops policies and practices that encourage and respond to the diverse expressions of gifts and talents in children. To this end, the QC/GT supports and engages in research and development, staff development, advocacy, communication and collaboration with other organisations and agencies who strive to improve the quality of education for all students. In addition, the QC/GT aims at:

- Promoting the development, implementation and evaluation in all schools of a coherent policy for gifted and talented children;
- Encouraging commitment to the personal, social and intellectual development of the child;
- Encouraging a broad, balanced and appropriate curriculum for gifted and talented children;
- Providing appropriate support, resources and materials for the education of gifted and talented children;
- Encouraging the use of a differentiated educational computerised provision in the classroom through curriculum enrichment and extension;
- Stimulating, initiating and co-ordinating research activities.

One of the most valuable features of the service provided by the QC/GT is the regular *Newsletter* which facilitates the sharing of information and good practice. In addition to the *Newsletter* and *Journal*, QC/GT produces an ever-increasing range of publications designed to help parents, teachers and other professionals.

Why should gifted education be supported?

This question is often asked in a confrontational manner by those who believe that gifted individuals do not need special educational provisions. Some sincerely feel that truly gifted children will remain gifted and fulfil their educational needs on their own. Others feel that if teachers are doing their job, the gifted should be able to get by without the special attention that other atypical learners need. The following are some ideas that those who hold such views must be asked to consider:

- Gifted and talented children must be given stimulating educational experiences appropriate to their level of ability if they are to realise their potential. Giftedness arises from an interaction between innate capabilities and an environment that challenges and stimulates to bring forth high levels of ability and talent.

- Each person has the right to learn and to be provided challenges for learning at the most appropriate level where growth proceeds most effectively.

- Traditional education currently does not sufficiently value bright minds.

- When given the opportunity gifted and talented students can use their vast amount of knowledge to serve as a background for unlimited learning.

Providing for our finest minds allows both individual and societal needs to be met. Contributions to society in all areas of human endeavour come in overweighted proportions from this population of individuals. Society needs the gifted adult to play a far more demanding and innovative role than that required of the more typical learner. We need integrated, highly functioning persons to carry out those tasks that will lead all of us to a satisfying, fulfilling future.

In the QC/GT, three enrichment programmes are provided for children from grade three up to grade twelve. These programmes are conducted on a part time withdrawal basis three afternoon sessions per week. The Enrichment Triad Model (see J Renzulli, ed.) has been implemented in a number of schools in Qatar. In addition, in special rooms within the school building, students work independently or are guided by a special resource teacher on freely chosen or assigned projects. It is now becoming possible for gifted and talented students in Qatar to 'skip grades'. After decades of neglect, both the conceptions of giftedness and creativity receive more attention in this state.

In Qatar, Dr Abdul Azuz al-Hor and his colleagues have established a new agenda for teaching science and mathematics as an active process of discovery and inquiry. Gifted and talented students are provided with curricular opportunities, provisions, and classroom practices to experience the delights of scientific and mathematical communication, reasoning, creative thinking and creative problem solving.

Subhi, T. (2001) *The Qatari Centre for the Gifted and Talented.* ECHA News, 15 (1), p 3-4. Reproduced with kind permission from Dr Subhi and ECHA News.

Social development of gifted children: fact and fiction

(Maureen Neihart, PsyD)

A popular view about gifted children is that they're socially immature. Even parents of gifted children themselves will sometimes comment about their child's social awkwardness. There are exceptions, of course, but generally, studies indicate that the social development (*ie* social problem solving, social understanding, and social skills) of intellectually gifted children is *advanced* compared to that of their age mates. People are sometimes surprised to hear this because it doesn't fit their perception.

Like many other aspects of development, social development follows mental age more closely than it does chronological age. Since gifted children are cognitively advanced, it's not surprising that they usually resemble children several years older more than they do their own age mates in regard to moral reasoning, expectations for friendships, identity formation, interests, play behaviour, problem solving, *etc*. Gifted children tend to advance through developmental milestones more quickly than do other children, often outpacing their classmates in many areas. Why, then, is the perception that they're social misfits so common?

The first, and perhaps most obvious reason is that gifted children are commonly grouped in school with children who match their chronological age, rather than their mental age. They spend the majority of their time with children who are dissimilar developmentally. As a result, their differences may be more noticeable and they may seem out of place.

Think about it. How would you do if you spent most of your time with nice people who were developmentally quite a bit younger than you, say, young adults? Their interests, attitudes, expectations, and abilities would be quite a bit different from yours. Would you want to make friends within that group? Close friends? How would you cope with the differences?

Many of us would have no problem with it and simply adapt, choosing not to share our ideas or interests that we knew were different. Some of us would become managers, maybe even be accused of being bossy or domineering, but we would get things done! We might be popular and admired or respected because of our competence. We might organise those we worked with, supervising, coordinating, and leading. Others of us would take a more passive, laid back approach in order to reduce our frustration. We'd do our part, but we'd be more observers or loners than leaders. A few of us might choose to withdraw, seeming aloof, not wanting to work with those from whom we felt so different. A minority among us might respond with hostility, venting our frustration and disappointment directly or indirectly onto colleagues or family members, or protecting ourselves from our perceived rejection with the armour of anger.

Gifted children who spend most of their learning time with age mates who have less ability, interest or drive, find ways to cope with the challenges, the isolation, and the frustration. You have probably observed gifted children with socially inappropriate behaviours who are able to function very well among a group of older children or adults, people with whom they are more similar. Since their social development is advanced, they manage quite well in a group of older people.

Another reason why gifted children are sometimes perceived as socially immature is because their development is asynchronous. Within any individual, different abilities develop at varying rates. Since gifted children's cognitive abilities are so advanced, the discrepancies between those and other abilities can sometimes be enormous. As a result, people may view the child as socially immature because his or her social behaviours don't meet the expectations adults have formed based on the child's cognitive abilities. "He thinks like a sixteen year old, why doesn't he relate like a sixteen year old?" Despite appearances, however, odds are good that the gifted child's social development is also advanced beyond that of his or her age mates. It's simply not as advanced as that of his or her mental abilities.

One of the best ways to promote healthy social development among gifted children is to help them locate and participate in a gifted cohort group. Do what you can to increase their access to true peers – people who are similar to them in interests, ability, and drive. Flexible cluster grouping in classrooms, for instance, is essential in schools where students of all abilities are taught together in the same classroom or where there are few accelerated classes. Clusters of at least five to seven gifted students in a classroom will increase the chances that a gifted child will have at least one classmate like him or herself.

There are some schools that still prefer to sprinkle gifted students throughout the classrooms so that each teacher gets one or two. This practice may satisfy the teachers, but it will probably be problematic for the gifted student! Research to date indicates that gifted students who have ready access to true peers have better adjustment than do those who must often work with others unlike themselves. The more advanced a student is, the more this seems be true. Advocate for cluster grouping in your child's school, and be prepared to help school personnel find ways to meet the needs of students of all abilities so that no practice exacts too high a price from certain groups.

Advanced classes, summer programmes designed specifically for gifted children, play groups with gifted children or with older children, high level extracurricular options, and other programmes that draw high ability children are avenues for increasing gifted children's access to people like themselves.

In summary, growing up gifted is different to what most children experience, and social development in particular is noticeably different for intellectually gifted children. It is not uncommon for a seven-year-old gifted child to be cognitively similar to a 12-year-old, socially similar to a nine-year-old, and physically just like other seven-year-olds. These developmental discrepancies present challenges for parents and child alike, but they are especially difficult to deal with when the child has limited access to true peers. Therefore, one of the most beneficial things we can do to support the healthy adjustment of our gifted children is make sure they have time to learn and play with others like themselves.

(Mureen Neihart, 2003, reprinted with kind permission of the author).

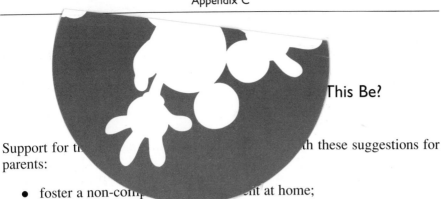

This Be?

Support for th[...]th these suggestions for parents:

- foster a non-com[...]nt at home;
- praise constantly;
- emphasise positive aspects of behaviour;
- criticise the behaviour, not the child;
- divide large tasks into small ones, so that the child can enjoy many successes;
- give specific instructions;
- encourage the child to become a collector, and thus the 'resident and class expert';
- prepare the child for new situations;
- know that your child will need support through plateaus and setbacks;
- be in touch with parents of other learning disabled children;
- keep in touch frequently with your child's Special Needs teacher and regular classroom teachers.

Lavoie, R (1989) *How Difficult Can This Be? F.A.T. City Workshop.* PBS Video, 1320 Braddock Place, Alexandria, Virginia 22314-1698. Reprinted with kind permission from Richard Lavoie.

Twelve management tips for children with ADHD

1. Big clock – big time: use timers to make time visible and time limits reasonable.

2. Be fast with praise: use short comments or quick soft touches as soon as possible.

3. Praise, praise, more praise: ADHD children need to know the facts about their behaviour that you like. ADHD children need praise more often than normal children to help them control or check their behaviour and increase their work output.

4. Be a slot-machine for quick, cheap, kid-valuable goodies: ADHD children seem to need more rewards that they can see or feel. These rewards need to be important to them.

5. Change the payoffs, be creative: try to keep the child from becoming bored with your reward list or cheap goodies. Change your payoffs or rewards.

6. Act don't yack: ADHD children have a problem behaving as you want. It is a performance problem, not a problem of understanding. Use comments, rewards, payoffs and outcomes swiftly and often, and reduce your repeating of rules, and verbal nagging or 'yakking'.

7. Be positive: state the wanted behaviour in a positive way. Decide what you want the child to be doing. Then tell the child what you want him to do. Set up a reward programme to encourage further growth of this behaviour. Discuss with your psychologist when the child responds with an unwanted behaviour. Punishment used first, and often, does not manage or control behaviour for long periods of time.

8. Scouts, be prepared!: ADHD children often have problems in the same situations over and over again. You are able to expect what settings or places your child's behaviour is difficult to manage or control. By preparing for these places you can plan to manage the problem before it occurs. You can decrease the chance of the problem starting. Before the child moves into a problem place, follow these five steps:

   • review 2-3 rules with the child, and post the rules as a visual reminder. Have the child repeat the rules back;

   • set up a small instant time-in or payoff for the child to get if they follow the rules;

   • set up a small instant outcome for disobeying the rules;

   • as you enter the situation, begin and then keep on giving the child attention (time-in) for good rule following or for being helpful;

   • give your outcomes at once upon seeing the welcome and/or unwelcome behaviours.

9. Keep a disability in mind: ADHD is a disorder that lessens your child's ability to stop themselves. These children are not able to self-manage their behaviour without help or training from others. This causes prob-

lems at home, school and other places where behaviours need to start or stop. This handicap is visible in the way your child has problems in controlling her/his behaviour and being on time. Also, many children meeting criteria for ADHD mature slower than their peers.

10. Pick your battles, make them few: rank what is important for you and your child. Remember, have goals with this child that have some social or growth importance. Know which battles to fight and which to leave alone. Do not lock horns with or be at odds with the child over unimportant or small misbehaviours.

11. Stop pointing! Don't blame self! Don't blame child!: Put distance between your adult problems and those of your child. Your ways will not work all the time with an ADHD child. ADHD children normally have periods of tough days and not so tough days. These changes are not related to how good you are at parenting, but part of your child's disability.

12. Be forgiving: at the end of each day, forgive the children their misbehaviour. Forgive others for their judging of you as you care for your child. Forgive yourself for the slips you are surely going to make in managing or directing such a child.

(Ward & Purvis, 1997)

The hidden dimension of learning: time and space

(Smith, 1998/1999)

Maria is a gifted graduate student studying toward a degree in social work. Her insight and her mastery of complex issues are superior. However, she is unable to complete papers for her coursework on time. Her professors claim that she is lazy, undisciplined, and even manipulative. When her cognitive abilities were tested, Maria's scores were in the gifted range. But her scores on The Test of Written Language placed her planning, organising, and sequencing abilities on a low seventh grade level.

David, a high school student, is late to all his classes. He has trouble going to bed on time at night and waking up in the morning, even with two alarm clocks. Donald has difficulty pacing himself and keeping track of time. His teachers think he is behaving this way on purpose to flout authority.

Annie's junior high school teachers call her "careless" and "scatter-brained" because she is always losing her homework, misplacing her backpack, and forgetting her gym clothes. They say she "needs to have her head reattached to her body" in order to get herself organised. They are very impatient with her and are now using a "demerit system" in an effort to impose order on her.

Max, a third grader, has been described as having a "faulty radar" because he always seems to end up in the wrong place at the wrong time, making his life and the lives of those around him very difficult. Max doesn't mean to, but he bumps into everyone, knocks things over, spills his milk and juice, and can't keep track of when it is his turn in games.

The problem that these individuals share is something that:

- Parents confront every morning when they try to help a child with learning disabilities get dressed and out the door for school;

- Teachers face when their students with learning disabilities cannot find their way to their next classroom, even after a month of school;

- Employers encounter when their intelligent employees with learning disabilities arrive late to work, and take too long to complete required tasks or eat lunch;

- Friends deal with when their friends with learning disabilities don't show up as promised and forget to call.

Individuals who struggle with issues of time and space often complain that their inner clocks are not working, their timing is off, they can't seem to pace themselves or self regulate during even familiar tasks, and they are "hopelessly lost" when tasks demand careful timing or call for a sense of space.

Most individuals acquire concepts of time and space naturally as they mature. But for those with learning disabilities, these skills don't always develop automatically and so they have to be learned. Learning disabilities can result in disorganisation which can be life-long and pervasive, starting in the preschool years and, often, continuing on through adulthood. By four years of age, most children have a good understanding of spatial words and know the meaning of terms such as 'beneath' and 'above,' 'near' and 'far,' 'under' and 'over,' and 'above' and 'below'. Confusing these terms can impede learning in such areas as reading, writing, math, geography, and even history.

Two organising systems of our society are space and time. Many people with learning disabilities have difficulties with spatial organisation. They have trouble distinguishing left from right. They have a poor sense of direction, misread maps, and have trouble following printed directions. They tend to get lost even in their own neighbourhoods. These individuals lack the 'internal maps' that most of us use to guide how we move our bodies through space and how we travel from one place to another. "When I get lost, which is frequently, I use my portable car phone," says a doctor who has both learning disabilities and Attention Deficit/Hyperactivity Disorder (ADHD). "I always try to park in the same parking lot and use the same two rows; otherwise I never can find my car when I come back. And I'm apt to lose my parking lot ticket, too!" Feelings of helplessness and frustration frequently overtake persons with learning disabilities who stand at crossroads, bewildered about which road might lead to a chosen destination.

The person with learning disabilities who gets lost in time has life disrupted even more severely than does a person who gets lost in space. Time regulates our waking hours with tyrannical force. The alarm clock wakes us at a precise time so that we can get to work on time. We schedule meetings and appointments throughout the day and calculate how long they will last so that we can make it to them all and still find time for lunch. We must leave work at a given time to catch a ride home, or pick up the kids, or run evening errands.

Problems for families

The child with learning disabilities who experiences problems with space often:

- has trouble finding belongings (school books, homework, keys, toys);
- is prone to getting lost in public places (supermarkets, department stores, libraries);
- has difficulty knowing how to adjust their behaviour in ways that demonstrate an appreciation of others' personal space.

This child will frequently have a room which everyone calls "the pit," with stuff piled on top of other things and little sense of organisation. However, the child will claim, "I know where everything is."

The child with learning disabilities who experiences problems with time often:

- can't seem to regulate his or her daily schedule;
- is late getting to and from places;
- has difficulty with the verbal timing of remarks that is important for effective communication and is essential to others' appreciation of a sense of humour;
- has trouble picking up the rhythm of conversations.

Problems in school

Two areas where teachers must provide structure in order for children to succeed in the classroom are space (a place for all things) and time (a time for each activity). Establishing order in these two areas will create the setting for productive learning to occur.

Creating order in space

Organising desk space is often a problem for those with learning disabilities where to put the work, where to work on it, and where to put it upon completion. They need help with:

- organising a notebook;
- organising a backpack;
- organising space on paper;
- following directions about spatial organisation.

Creating structure in time

Students may have difficulty:

- with the organisation of the school day;
- with rhyming, syllabication, and breaking down sounds in words;
- handing in work on time or completing assignments in an allotted time-frame;
- planning free time;
- with timed tests;
- with long-term assignments (research or book reports; science projects).

Poor time management can cause great difficulties in the school, work, home, and social environments. One young man, Andrew, said, "You know my reading and spelling didn't cause me half the trouble my stupid left-right mix up and my getting lost and being late did. It was the night before the due date on the exam when I got to work. I never thought about time. I lost a lot of jobs because I was late and I couldn't figure out how long it would take me to do various jobs." Disorganisation in time and space causes problems for friends, roommates, or life-partners (meeting people in the right place at the right time, paying bills on time, keeping an orderly home).

Disorganisation in time and space can make a person feel rotten!

Lacking an accurate internal sense of time and space, a person with learning disabilities may race through the day, feeling out of control and rebounding from one activity to the next. It's as if time and space don't happen to this person! These individuals find themselves missing appointments, quitting classes and jobs, changing rooming arrangements, and being lost. Having an internal clock that isn't working right can make one feel like he or she is on the fringes of society. "I always feel out of it," says Clara, "because I come after they have started class, I don't catch up to them even when they leave, and what I am left with is a dismal sense of failure."

Working towards solutions

We have to present children with activities that help with categorisation and classification (sorting objects and pictures, then symbols) in ways that correspond with their chronological ages, developing abilities, personal interests and increasing maturity. By working on their skills in grouping things together, and by expanding their understanding of relationships between items, we help them build strong mental 'filing systems,' so that well-organised information can be retrieved easily.

Children with learning disabilities tend to learn best by doing, touching, seeing, hearing, feeling; in other words, they need to learn through experience. An often overlooked means of helping children to grow in these areas is through movement and activities that involve perceptual motor skills. Learning to use their bodies in a more organised way will help them to use their minds in a more organised manner. For example:

- music helps build rhythm and timing. A drumbeat can help reinforce syllabication in reading;

- floor maps walked on or hopped over can help teach geography;

- time lines that can be walked on can help children gain a better understanding of history by placing events in an understandable time-frame;

- elastic or rope can help children understand angles and geometric forms.

People with learning disabilities and ADHD who have difficulties with their sense of time and space can be helped to overcome their difficulties and to lead productive and fulfilling lives.

Smith, S (1998/1999) 'The Hidden Dimension of Learning: Time and Space'. *Their World,* National Council of Learning Disabilities, New York. Reproduced with kind permission from Sally Smith and *Their World.*

Sally L Smith is the Founder/Director of The Lab School of Washington and Baltimore. She is a professor in charge of the Graduate Program in Special Education/Learning Disabilities in the School of Education, American University, in Washington, DC, and is a former member of the Professional Advisory Board of NCLD.

When the words are there but the hand won't write

Washington – Back when I was an investigative reporter, Vice President Spiro Agnew subpoenaed my notes. Mr Agnew, under investigation for bribery and tax evasion, alleged that the Justice Department was trying to drive him from office by leaking false information to the press. Like other reporters subpoenaed, I handed my notes over to my lawyer. Unlike the others, though, I was confident no one would ever read them. That is because not even I could read my notes. I was – I am – learning disabled.

When I was a kid, there was no such thing as learning disabled. There was 'dumb' or its middle-class variant, 'underachiever'. (Poor kids are never underachievers, since they are not expected to achieve much to begin with.) My disability has to do with small-motor coordination: I cannot write. Of course, writing is what I do for a living. But that writing has always been on a typewriter and, now, a word processor. It is writing with a pencil or pen that I am talking about. Even under the best circumstances, I can't do it well. My handwriting is illegible. I write slowly, painfully and always sloppily. I cannot write a simple thank-you note, and it has been years since I have even attempted one. I type everything.

As learning disabilities go, mine is not catastrophic. It did mean that in school I had a hard time with essays. The ideas in my head could not find their way onto paper. I was slow where others were fast. And where neatness counted, as it almost always did, I was judged lacking and told that it was my own fault. The field of education is resplendent with jargon. But 'learning disabled' is not jargon. It means that accommodations must be made, that rules or procedures must be waived, that a child or adult must be treated as an individual. If he or she cannot learn in the standard way, new ways must be found. In my case, a typewriter did the trick. I took a typing course in high school and it changed my life. Words and phrases that once I could not get down on paper burst from the typewriter. The phrase 'neatness counts' no longer chilled, and I wrote and wrote and wrote.

Years later, a psychologist told me that I had – have! – a learning disability. At first I was stunned: Me? Learning disabled? Then my shock turned to anger – anger at all the teachers who never recognised my problem, who insisted that I do things their way. Then I got angry about all those other kids with more severe learning disabilities, those who were told they were dumb or lazy when they were in fact learning disabled. In some cases, they were asked to do what they simply could not do. It is certain that some handicapped kids were made to feel dumb. Call a kid dumb and he'll oblige. Call him an underachiever and he will not achieve. You can learn much from a teacher. I have written this column for a reason. The other night, I heard two teenagers refer to a girl as an LD. In their mouths, the term was descriptive, not at all pejorative, and I was pleased that, at least with the young, the concept of learning disabilities has gained acceptance. I thought of myself and also thought about how once before, I had written on their subject. The mother of a learning disabled boy called to thank me. She had given the column to her son and it lifted his spirits. There are prizes galore in my business, but none better than that.

Cohen, R. (1987). 'When the Words Are There But the Hand Won't Write'. *International Herald Tribune,* Washington Post Writers Group, Washington DC, June 12 issue. Reproduced with kind permission from the Washington Post Writers Group.

Standardised tests: still an essential option for international schools

A recent editorial in *The International Educator*, 'Standardised testing dies hard,' argues that international schools should abandon standardised tests. This argument is very popular right now, but one that is not supported by psychometric evidence, research, or facts. Before international schools embrace the move to abandon standardised achievement tests (group or individually administered), we believe that it is important that they examine the evidence surrounding the testing debate and consider the implications of such abandonment.

Standardised tests have stood the test of time for some very good reasons. First and foremost, such tests have been shown to be the fairest, most reliable, bias-free and valid form of assessment available. Their objective scoring procedures and standardised formats, often the focus of criticism, are the very characteristics that ensure their validity and fairness. Most importantly, the objectivity and standardisation of the tests safeguard students from the effects of stereotypes, preconceptions, and other biases.

No psychometrician worth her salt would claim that standardised tests are flawless, only that they are enormously useful and far better than their proposed replacements. Numerous reports on statewide, as well as national, attempts to move to alternative assessments confirm their inadequacy relative to standardised testing programmes. For example, a 1993 issue of *PHI DELTA KAPPAN* chronicled Great Britain's disappointing experiment with 'authentic testing'. Most recently, the state of Kentucky returned to standardised, multiple-choice achievement tests after a brief and unhappy experience with more 'authentic' assessment. Kentucky's return to traditional assessment, reported in the Jan/Feb 1996 issue of *The Harvard Education Letter*, was prompted by concerns about the validity and fairness of the new assessments, as well as instances of teachers helping students to 'augment' their portfolios. The problems with alternative assessments was summarised in a 1995 *Science* article where the author states that: 'Studies of state testing programs show that the new tests do not reduce methodological problems, they increase them. The scoring is unreliable and measures of validity are lacking.'

Although some new instruments show promise, overall, the evidence clearly shows that performance-based, non-standardised testing programmes are more expensive, more time-consuming, less reliable and less valid than the standardised tests they were designed to replace. In addition, the most frequently recommended forms of alternative assessment are inherently open to the very real possibility of inaccurate and unfair evaluation because of subjective scoring procedures.

Aside from their reliability, fairness, and efficiency, there are other compelling reasons for international schools to use standardised tests. If a school wants to make meaningful comparisons across schools, classrooms, time, conditions, or curricula, a standard measure is needed. Standardised tests provide a comparability yardstick, perspective, the 'big picture'. As educators, important decisions about instruction or curriculum should not be based solely on the information we gain from locally generated feedback.

None of us would want our personal physician certified to practice medicine based on a test developed by the medical school she attended.

If there are good, sound reasons to keep standardised tests as one option in a school's assessment arsenal, why then the impassioned plea to abandon them? Is it that such tests represent 'the control or accountability imposed from without?' Is it the sense that an outside authority is judging local efforts? Certainly, the 'high-stakes' environments within which standardised tests have been used in the states have contributed to the defensiveness surrounding them. Since standardised tests are the most effective and valid instruments we have for accountability purposes, it is probably understandable that they would be the target of so much criticism. But, in international schools where the education offered is often far superior to that available in a stateside school, one wonders why there would be resistance to documenting this superiority.

Another explanation for the antagonism towards standardised tests could be the many instances of misuse (*eg*, coaching students, repeated testings with identical forms). Such abuses, however, are not limited to standardised assessments. Performance-based, 'authentic' assessments can also be misused. In addition to Kentucky's experience with cheating, teachers in Maryland recently were charged with helping students to cheat on a performance-based test. Although unfortunate, these instances of irresponsible behaviour are not a reflection on the tests themselves, but on the individuals using the test or the context within which the tests are administered. The answer, obviously, is not to reject a potentially useful tool because of the risk of misuse, but rather to weed out irresponsible use and interpretation of tests through education and vigilance.

Understandably, international schools have specific concerns and issues surrounding the use of standardised tests that are legitimate and require examination. For example, the possibility that standardised tests contain socially and culturally biased items would certainly be a reason to question their use with student populations that are culturally diverse. And yet, an examination of most standardised achievement tests will reveal very few, if any, culture-specific items. The reason for this is that large testing companies are particularly vigilant about finding and eliminating items that could be interpreted as biased against any group, including gender groups. They also have a mechanism in place to remove items with psychometric properties that differ for gender, ethnic or cultural groups.

Of course, any test published in English should not be given to students whose English is so poor that they would be unable to read and understand the items. For the majority of students attending international schools, however, who are expected to perform day-to-day in an English-speaking environment, the usual standardised test should be entirely appropriate.

International schools also have the option to allow for some flexibility in their use of standardised tests. For example, if a particular test item is found that contains wording or information that would be unfamiliar to a child or group of children, a test administrator could either provide the child with the cultural context for the item or reject that particular item. Of course, any deviation from standard procedure should be considered when interpreting the child's test score. Another option is for international schools to develop local norms that may be more meaningful for their community and that could supplement norms provided by the test developer. What we are suggesting is that any test (whether standardised or not) should be used with common sense, as well as discretion.

Another troubling claim is that standardised tests are unfair to the most educationally disadvantaged and least well-served of our student population. The truth is that these groups have the most to lose by the demise of a practice that offers protection against biased and unfair assessment triggered by a child's ethnic or cultural background. If a particular child or group of children are scoring poorly on a standardised measure, instead of blaming the test, it is important to consider that there may be something missing in their educational experience that calls for intervention. One of the most important benefits derived from standardised tests may be as an indicator of systemic problems that have the most negative impact on the very students some would like to protect from the 'insidious practice' of standardised assessment.

The claim that the content of current tests is not representative or comprehensive of what is taught in international schools is interesting, but also puzzling. First, no good standardised measure should be a perfect reflection of any individual curriculum. Standardised tests are useful precisely because they are not tied to any one curriculum, but rather hone in on what should be at the core of all. After all, no matter how idiosyncratic a school's curriculum, parents should have some assurance that there is a set of knowledge and skills contained in that curriculum to ensure that their child is adequately prepared to move from system-to-system or country-to-country. This would seem to be particularly important for an international school population.

Finally, standardised tests were never designed to assess everything a school might teach a student. Rather, the intent is to provide a general assessment of the most important skills, information, and concepts from a given academic area. Among such core content tested by standardised assessments is the ability to comprehend written passages, reason quantitatively, do calculations, understand correct language usage, and express oneself in writing. In addition, contrary to what some critics have claimed, good multiple-choice tests also require the use of inferential, analytic and synthetic skills. Of course, a school might go beyond core concepts and skills. And, this should be assessed as well to give a complete picture of a child's learning.

In the end, we believe that alternative assessment has the potential to enrich and expand the nature of information that current tests provide. However, as noted by a leading expert on evaluation methodology, "the success of the alternative testing movement will not depend on how effectively its most passionate firebrands carry out a scorched earth campaign against standardised testing, rather, the success of the movement will depend on the validity of its internal rationale, as well as how the alternative measures meet criteria established by testing professionals and standards set by test consumers".

Standard and non-standard, locally and nationally developed tests provide different information and accomplish different ends. Together they can give a fairer, more complete and, ultimately, more useful assessment of what our schools know and what they need to learn next.

Mills, C J & Durden, W G (1996) *Standardised Tests: Still an Essential Option for International Schools,* The International Educator, X (4) p 1,6.

Reproduced with kind permission from The International Educator, <http://www.tieonline.com>

Carol J Mills, PhD, head of Research, Institute for the Academic Advancement of Youth (IAAY) at The Johns Hopkins University. William G Durden, PhD, Executive Director of IAAT at The Johns Hopkins University and currently President of Dickinson College, Carlisle, Pennsylvania.

Appendix D

Case studies

Laura (gifted): a seventh grade student at an international school was found to be a very good writer. This was the result of the school's screening of all students from the third grade through high school with the Test of Written Language-3. Laura received the highest score in the school. Her story was creative and way above the level expected of a seventh grade student. Her English teacher immediately began to search for outlets for this talent. She encouraged Laura to send in stories to various literary magazines, which eventually published her work. She also helped Laura to apply for the Johns Hopkins International Talent Search, which requires students to take the SAT reasoning tests to qualify for the university's summer and distant learning programmes. The teacher's aim was for Laura to be identified as a gifted writer and be followed by a real author through the Hopkins writing programme for creative writers through a distance learning experience. Here is what Laura's mother wrote to Laura's teacher after the family had returned to the United States. "Thank you for all your efforts on Laura's behalf. She received the SGIS Literary Magazine last week and found one of her stories had been published. It was a thrill to see her written words published. We also must update you on the Johns Hopkins program. Laura took the SAT in January. She scored 550 on the Verbal part and 550 in the Math part. We thought these scores were high. Well, Johns Hopkins confirmed this assessment with a letter stating Laura is accepted into their program with scores in the top 2% in Laura's age group! Her scores were higher than the average 17 year old. The most exciting part is Laura now has an opportunity to get additional help in writing. If it had not been for your help at the international school, she would not have been identified. So your efforts may help lead Laura into a career in writing. You have made a real difference for Laura. We called our local university which has a Talent Search to see if Laura could attend a creative writing class. They have a two week writing class given by a teacher who has received great reviews. We thought a live teacher would be better the first time rather than a tutorial course. She may still do the tutorial course this summer also. Again, thank you for taking such a keen interest in Laura. We are sure that your efforts have started her on her writing career."

Authors' comments

We encourage your 6th through 8th grade students, who score at or above the 97th percentile rank on a standardised achievement test, to apply for the Johns Hopkins International Talent Search. You will find the Johns Hopkins website in the Appendix E: *Resources* section of this book. Not only will your students, who qualify for the programmes, be enchanted and enriched with the programmes, they will also be able to place this qualification on their university/college applications.

James (Dyslexic/ESL, 24 years old): Dear Mrs. ………. I am sorry that it took me along time to send you this exersise back, I hope you appreciate my excuse. Thank you for the report. After knowing you I dont think me life will be the same any more.. becase now I know that I am like every body els but I need more time to do certen thing. I thank you very much for your encaragment and support, and your time. By the way, this is the first letter that I write with out using the dectionery and with out rewriting it another time. I wont be ashamed of my spelling misstakes, that is the way I was born. Thank you again, and looling forward to seeing you. With kind regard, James

Authors' comments

It is unfortunate that this young man had to wait so long and to suffer throughout his schooling to be tested and identified as dyslexic. This is why we beg you to apply some of the suggestions from our book to your existing or introduction of a Learning Resource Centre.

Roberta (gifted, dyslexic, ADHD): Roberta entered school for the first time as a third grade student at an international school. It was immediately observed that she appeared easily distracted, agitated (restless), spoke out whenever she wanted and frequently got out of her seat to walk around the classroom. She could not pay attention more than about two minutes or keep on task for more than about two minutes. She refused to hold a pencil or crayon in her hand or use scissors, and it became apparent that she could not write her numbers, add or subtract, write the alphabet or words. She could read about two years above her age and had a vast vocabulary and general knowledge. She was immediately placed with the school's special education teacher where she began remediation for her difficulties and enrichment for her strengths. She also continued to be mainstreamed for areas where she could cope. Testing was requested for Roberta, and it was found that she had visual-motor co-ordination difficulties, might be dyslexic in spelling and mathematics, was intellectually gifted in the verbal skills and showed symptoms (DSM IV and other criteria) of ADHD. The definitive diagnosis of dyslexia was postponed for re-testing after she had had about a year of formal instruction as she had been home-schooled and allowed to learn what she wanted to learn which was definitely not pencil and paper activities. Roberta was referred to a paediatrician for the medical diagnosis of ADHD and was indeed described as a clear case of ADHD, and the doctor recommended medication (Ritalin) to help this medical problem. Roberta's parents refused medication for Roberta. Roberta's behaviour within the regular classroom did not improve with time in a formal education environment, and after many consultations from the staff involved with Roberta and her parents, Ritalin was again recommended by the school to try to help Roberta begin to focus. Her parents refused over and over again, and were not willing to permit a trial of medication even for one week. One year later, Roberta was re-tested, and it was found that she was dyslexic in the written work – spelling and mathematics. Her ability to focus and pay attention had not improved, and it was thought that her pace of learning had regressed. The suggestion of Ritalin was again proposed for Roberta, but again her parents refused stating, "We do not want our daughter's perceptual abilities, orientation or creativity affected by the results of Ritalin. We want our daughter to correct her perceptions, to visualise and picture things using her imagination without being drugged." Although Roberta's parents had been thoroughly briefed about medication for ADHD and had received articles from the New England Journal of Medicine and American Academy of Pediatrics about testing and the possible benefits of medication, Roberta's parents continued to refuse a trial of medication. Apparently Roberta's parents had read articles for and against the use of medications for ADHD from an internet site which advertises a treatment for dyslexia and had decided to go with the non-medication approach rather than take the advice of the school, testing report and paediatrician. A few months later, Roberta had begun to have behavioural problems, had greater difficulties with attention and concentration, and had progressed at a much slower pace academically than what would be expected of an individual correctly treated for ADHD and with such superb intelligence. Her special education lessons for dyslexia were impeded by Roberta's inability to pay attention to the instructions and to remain on task. The last words for this situation were summed up to Roberta's parents by the school's special education teacher, "I hope that Roberta will improve, and I really want this for her, but be prepared for her to learn about Ritalin as a teenager or young woman. She might ask you why you did not at least try the medication for her and not let her suffer as much as she did throughout her entire school life".

Authors' comments

We think this case shows that we cannot always succeed in trying to place our values on parents even if we think we are correct in what we are recommending. We logged on to the Internet site the parents used as proof for refusing medication for Roberta. Indeed we found the exact words that her parents used on the site, and to paraphrase another statement, the site stated that they require that their clients be medication free in order to follow the programme of treating dyslexia. We made e-mail contact with the programme director, and in our second e-mail to him, we asked for the research to base up their claims that creativity, visualisation, perceptual abilities, orientation and that the central nervous system are all negatively affected by taking Ritalin. Our e-mail request remains unanswered to date.

ADHD case studies- presentations of ADHD in adolescents

"It is common for teenagers to present for evaluation of possible ADHD at major life transition points such as entry into middle school, high school, or college. The pediatrician must be able to document the presence of the core symptoms of the disorder before age 10 to make a positive diagnosis, even if no impairment occurred during childhood. Those individuals who displayed physical hyperactivity or conduct problems as part of their presentation of ADHD have usually been identified before adolescence because their disruptive behaviour in school and at home is difficult to overlook. Individuals who present for evaluation in adolescence are more likely to:

- be primarily inattentive;
- have mental rather than physical restlessness;

- have high IQ;

- reside in highly supportive families who helped them compensate for their deficits earlier in life. More often than not, girls are referred later than boys for evaluation.

The following two vignettes illustrate such presentations.

Case study #1

Fourteen-year-old Sarah was a highly social young adolescent who got along well with her family. Teachers found Sarah charming and often over-looked her chronic tardiness with school assignments, accepted her creative excuses for incomplete work, mistook her extrovert verbal style for high intellectual ability, and did not discipline her for socialising instead of doing written work during class. Although she coasted through elementary school with satisfactory grades, the increasing demands for organisation and long-term planning inherent in the middle school curriculum proved overwhelming. By the middle of eighth grade, she was in danger of failing, coming to class unprepared, inconsistently completing homework and, when she did it, often losing homework before class or turning it in late.

Her parents were surprised by these academic problems. In the past, Sarah had always done well in school. Although they acknowledged that she was a 'total slob' and an 'air head' at home, they always had viewed her as a capable student, just a bit 'flighty'. A comprehensive psychological evaluation revealed that Sarah had ADHD. Because she was not disruptive and did well academically before middle school, no one suspected ADHD.

Case study #2

Bill was a gifted, artistically inclined 18-year-old college freshman with a full scale IQ of 135 who presented for evaluation because he was failing all of his college courses and had been placed on academic probation. Bill had attended private elementary, middle, and high schools for gifted youngsters, where he distinguished himself with outstanding painting, sculpture, and participation in drama. He received Cs and an occasional B in most academic subjects, where he rarely completed homework but managed to slide by because of his outstanding artistic talent and his ability to pass tests without studying. Upon arriving at college, he experienced overwhelming difficulty managing his time, completing academic work, and keeping up with the requirements. He did not study for examinations or complete papers on time, devoting most of this time to socialising and artistic pursuits. During the winter holiday after his first semester, his parents took him for a comprehensive evaluation, which resulted in a diagnosis of ADHD.

Sarah and Bill both had a childhood onset of ADHD symptoms, but these symptoms did not create significant impairment, resulting in referral and evaluation until middle or late adolescence. Sarah's charming personality and supportive environment helped her to succeed academically until she got to middle school. Bill got by on sheer brilliance and artistic talent until he reached college when the need to organise and persist at tasks overwhelmed him. In such cases, a complete history is central to establishing the correct diagnosis"

(Robin, 1999 p1027-1038).
Reproduced with kind permission of the author.

Ted (ADHD) High School Student: Ted's Miracle (written by his mother, 2002) 'Ted is faring extremely well. He is still able to concentrate very effectively in class and take notes without losing focus. He cannot only focus on class activities, but he is now capable of participating in class discussions and answering questions correctly and at times... brilliantly. Teachers have begun to give him positive comments. He has greatly reduced the amount of time it takes him to do homework and he is now able to finish tests in class, which he was not always capable of before. He is on the heels of a very difficult week, a sort of 'acid test' for him. He had very comprehensive tests and assignments all last week and normally he would have been overwhelmed by such daunting challenges, but he scheduled his time well and felt that he had done a good job of all the tests and projects and had learned a great deal. We don't have any of the results back yet, but we should get them in a day or two. Also, his semester grades come out in mid February. Ted seems more talkative and more confident, more assertive and much more motivated. He does seem to have a bit of an edge at times now, but it could be just the adjustment to the medication. I know that he is tired. He is doing so much more work now than he ever has (since he wasn't capable of intensive work before), that I think he has been exhausted from the effort. Things are slowing down now after last week though. Finally, he doesn't procrastinate anymore on homework assignments. He can get right down to work. We have left him completely alone to do all of his work on his own. There is no parent re-teaching of material or help. His difficulty in getting to sleep at night does seem to be disappearing, but he hasn't regained his former appetite yet. I think he is losing some weight, but we're still trying to prepare his favourite meals. I'm also looking into getting him some of those milkshake concoctions for weight gain. These are small sacrifices for his newfound confidence and apparently improved performance.

If you need any more information, please let me know. We know that Ted has some old habits he may have to alter in order to take full advantage of his newly released talents, but really he seems to be fully capable of performing well, even without any behavioural work or counselling. It's as if he has been learning for years how to succeed, but he just wasn't able. He truly doesn't seem to be lacking in skills such as organisation, writing compositions, researching projects, self-pacing, study techniques, *etc*. At times he can be lazy about chores, but not very often these days about schoolwork. Today Ted woke up too late to take his Ritalin and we wanted him to go to bed early tonight, so he didn't take any today. Well, the same old things started to happen. We had to remind him a million times to do things. He got angry, we got angry. He felt defensive and we felt worried. He wasn't as aware of anything, not even of the fact that his day was unproductive and he was not very nice. It brought back some pretty bad memories, and made us realise how our lives are a million times getter now.

I forgot to tell you perhaps the most important of the new developments. That is, he now enjoys school. He will actually say that he had a terrific day or that he enjoyed a class so much that he didn't want it to end. This is a radical departure from the past ... when he didn't even want to go to school and hated the experience. Also, weeks at home at homework time were hellish. Now, he is working hard, but he is the master of his destiny and there is no controversy.'

Dear teachers (written by Ted's parents for a parent-teacher conference),

There are many different symptoms of ADD, but typically ADD students are seen as *lazy, daydreaming* and *underachievers* by their teachers. Your assessments of Ted over the time that you have worked with him are largely consistent with this view. Specifically, these are the symptoms of ADD that Ted manifests :

1. Easy distractibility, trouble or inability to focus attention, tendency to 'tune out', drift away (so absorbs very little material from class).

2. Difficulty understanding and following through on instructions.

3. Tendency to work very slowly, so that finishing tasks or tests in class, a highly distracting environment, is a problem. Homework often takes numerous hours with scant learning. (He has qualified for having extra time on tests based on his recent diagnosis.).

4. Difficulty getting organised.

5. Chronic procrastination, difficulty knowing how or where to start.

6. Frequently frustrated or confused by his lack of success because, though very intelligent and intuitive, he can't tap into his own resources.

7. Because of rapid fire processing, will often skip information or steps.

8. Wildly inconsistent (performance depends on stimuli or distractions of the day).

He has struggled with these for the past 10 years at school and has only recently been competently assessed and diagnosed. He is now taking Ritalin, which has helped with his problem. We have already noticed following changes. From our perspective and Ted's, he is now better able to:

1. concentrate in conversations and express his opinions;

2. concentrate in class (he reports);

3. take notes in class and still concentrate on the matter at hand;

4. understand and follow instructions;

5. focus on and finish assignments in a reasonable amount of time;

6. understand material in class and retain it;

7. have confidence in his capabilities.

While the Ritalin has helped, it is not a miracle cure and Ted will still have his good days and his bad days. He is going through a fair amount of remedial tutoring to make up academic ground lost when he was less able to concentrate and learn. He is trying diligently to change habits which have persisted for years. He is determined to succeed but desperately needs encouragement and support, especially from you. He is at times quite exhausted from all this additional work and the fact that the Ritalin makes it difficult to sleep. So please have a little patience, offer whatever encouragement you can and keep this new information in mind when assessing his performance.

Authors' comments

The authors believe that proper training of all teachers in recognising the signs of ADHD is essential to international schools where students frequently change schools. The signs (see Chapter 6, *Programme delivery and accountability* and Appendices C, D and E) are pertinent to ESL students as well as native English speakers. It is important for teachers to be on the outlook for any signs of ADHD, learning disabilities, and/or gifted and talented as a normal practice of providing the appropriate instruction to meet students' educational needs. The authors also advise that international school heads state strongly to the staff that their personal opinions about medication for ADHD should remain private and not used to confuse and frighten parents who already feel concerned about medication for their child. The authors have seen this happen at international schools where teachers or staff were not informed about ADHD and caused great damage with their ignorance of the subject. This is a medical problem and only a physician has the right to follow the child; and teachers, associations or organisations do not have the right to suggest that parents take their child off medication for ADHD.

Mary (PTSD): Mary, a resource teacher at an international school was injured in an aeroplane accident. She returned to her job having been diagnosed and treated for PTSD, neck and back injuries mild enough to continue working. Mary felt that she had learned a lot about trauma and found that her work with Special Needs students took on an additional meaning as she could relate to some of her students' problems from her own problems dealing with PTSD (*eg* difficulties with short-term memory and concentration). She was able to help a set of parents whose daughter was in a similar accident with counselling and giving them information about PTSD. However, with this particular set of parents, although they suggested to their daughter that she might profit from an examination for PTSD, their daughter adamantly refused treatment. This was unfortunate as she became anorexic and began taking street drugs. Her excuse for not wanting to be examined and treated for PTSD was that she could not face the idea that she might have to talk about or experience again the anxiety she felt after the accident. It is not known what happened to this particular girl as she graduated from high school and apparently enrolled at university. But it is well known that without proper treatment for PTSD she might begin in the future to experience difficulties in her life such as depression, alcoholism, drug addiction, recurrent nightmares and problems with relationships.

Authors' comments

It is recommended that teachers and administrators learn more about PTSD as there may be children at international schools who have experienced the trauma of war, various accidents and events, which may have placed them in a PTSD type of mental difficulty.

Joan (Downs Syndrome): Class Six Reflections... My first impression was, "Watch Out!" I don't know why. Now she's a normal classmate just like everyone else and a great friend. What's the big deal? Joan has Downs

Syndrome, she may look just a little different and think a bit different but she deserves to be treated just like everyone else…why not?! I've learned not to be afraid of people with problems like Joan's. Don't be; it's no big deal. I've learned that they are just like you and me. When I first met Joan I was a bit nervous. Now Joan and I are great buddies. You just treat her with tolerance and respect; just like anyone else. What's the problem? I would like to say that people should stop treating Joan like a six-year-old child. Just because she has a bit of a difficulty it doesn't mean she's that different! Take my advice, Joan is more co-operative than anyone else when you treat her like anyone else. Joan has a great sense of humour; she can be really funny. One of the nicest moments I've ever had was when I went to the cinema with Joan. Joan can do just about everything we can do, from sports to art. It is difficult sometimes to get her to do stuff she doesn't want to do. But we can all be a bit stubborn sometimes. Everyone has the right to an education according to the United Nations. There's no reason why kids like Joan should be stopped from coming to school with normal kids. Besides, what's normal anyway?! Sometimes Joan can be a bit irritating; that's because she has a crush on me and I can't escape. I've known her since class 4. She's got a great sense of humour and is a great actress. She'll be on MTV one day. She's also really lucky to have such nice and loving parents. She sees the world a bit differently to us. Lucky Joan. Joan doesn't want special attention. She wants to be just like one of us. My advice? If she bothers you just ignore her but watch out she's stubborn and won't give in for some time! I've learned to be a little more patient, firm but gentle. I've also learned what responsibility and sharing really means. I will miss being around Joan. To tell the truth, I've enjoyed the year with Joan and she has changed a LOT. I will miss to have her around. You don't need to have Downs Syndrome to be shy. I'm shy and I'm meant to be 'normal?! I think I've been lucky to be with Joan this year. I've learned a lot about kids with 'special needs' and a lot about myself. I'll miss her next year. The year with Joan has been really cool … well, what can I say!

Joan' has gone on from this school to train as a classroom assistant under the supervision of the education department of the local university. The other students are continuing their education in the international schools.

Authors' comments

The concept of 'mainstreaming' children with very specific learning needs into international schools is one that has proved to be extremely effective. In this school, the children receive individual instruction by a qualified Special Needs teacher and are also part of the mainstream class. Much of the research has focused on the benefits gained by the child with 'Special Needs'. However, the benefits gained by the 'mainstream' children are immense. As can be seen by the comments above, the children have had a learning experience that is difficult to timetable and one that will remain with them for the rest of their lives. One way of mainstreaming very special needs children can be found in an article: *A Very Special International Education* (Hollington, 1994).

Appendix E

Resources

Attention Deficit Hyperactivity Disorder

Barley, RA & Murphy, KR (1998). *Attention-Deficit Hyperactivity Disorder: A Clinical Workbook.* New York: The Guilford Press.

Baum, S M, Olenchak, F R & Owen, S V (1998). Gifted Students with Attention Deficits: Fact and/or Fiction? Or, Can We See the Forest for the Trees? *Gifted Child Quarterly*, 42 (2), p96-104.

Bramer, J (1996). *Succeeding in College with Attention Deficit Disorders: Issues & Strategies for Students, Counselors, & Educators.* Florida: Specialty Press, Inc. ISBN 1-886941-06-8.

Cohen, M W (1998). *The Attention Zone: A Parent's Guide to Attention Deficit/Hyperactivity Disorder.* London: Brunner/Mazel.

Levine, M (2002). *A Mind at a Time.* New York: Simon & Schuster. ISBN 0-7432-02228.

Levine, M (1993). *All Kinds of Minds: A Young Student's Book about Learning Abilities and Learning Disorders.* Cambridge, MA: Educators Publishing Service, Inc. ISBN 0-8388-2090-5.

Levine, M (1994). *Educational Care: A System for Understanding and Helping Children with Learning Problems at Home and in School.* Cambridge, MA: Educators Publishing Service.

Levine, M (1988). *Explaining Attention Deficits to Children: The Concentration Cockpit.* Educators Publishing Service, Inc. 75 Moulton St., Cambridge, MA 02138-1104. ISBN 0-8388-1991-5.

Levine, M (1990). *Keeping a Head in School: A Student's Book about Learning Abilities and Learning Disorders.* Cambridge, MA: Educators Publishing Service, Inc. ISBN 0-8388-2069-7.

Pfiffner, L (1996). *All About ADHD: The Complete Practical Guide for Classroom Teachers.* Scholastic Professional Books, 555 Broadway, New York, NY 10012. ISBN 0-590-25108-2.

Rief, S (1993). *How to Reach and Teach ADD/ADHD Children.* The Centre for Applied Research in Education, West Nyack, New York, 10995.

Centres

Centre for Applied Special Technology (CAST) (2002). Universal Design for Learning for computer software, internet tools, and learning models for people of all ages with learning disabilities, physical challenges, and sensory impairments, as well as people who are typical learners or have extraordinary capabilities. 39 Cross

Street, Peabody, MA, USA 01960. Telephone: 001-978-531-8555, Fax: 001-978-531-0192, e-mail: cast@cast.org

Center for Talented Youth (CTY) (2002). The Johns Hopkins University, 3400 N. Charles Street, Baltimore, MD 21218, USA, Tel: 410-516-0278, Fax: 410-516-0377.

Center for Talented Youth Ireland (CTYI). Dublin City University, Dublin 9, Ireland. Tel: ++353-1-7005693, Fax: ++353-1-7005693.

National Research Centre on the Gifted and Talented, University of Connecticut, Tel: ++860-486-6265, Fax:++862-486-2900 <http:www.gifted.ucon.edu>

Emotional and Behaviour Disorders

Algozzine, B & Kay, P (2001). *Preventing Problem Behaviours: A Handbook of Successful Prevention Strategies*. Education Catalogue, Paul Chapman Publishing, 6 Bonhill Street, London EC2A 4PU, UK. ISBN 0-7619-7776-7.

Dowling, M (2000). *Young Children's Personal, Social and Emotional Development*. Education Catalogue, Paul Chapman Publishing, 6 Bonhill Street, London EC2A 4PU, UK. ISBN 0-7619-6360-X.

Hilton, A & Ringlaben, R (eds) (1998). *Best and Promising Practices in Developmental Disabilities*. Reston, VA: CEC Catalogue, The Council for Exceptional Children. ISBN 0-89079-720.

Hoover, J & Patton, J (1997). *Curriculum Adaptations for Students with Learning and Behaviour Problems: Principles and Practices*. Reston, VA: CEC Catalogue, The Council for Exceptional Children. ISBN 0-890-686-6

Lazarus, P (1996). *Trauma and Children: A Parent Handout for helping Children Heal*. National Association of School Psychologists. Miami, FL: Florida International University.

Perren-Klingler, G (ed.)(1996). *TRAUMA-From Individual Helplessness to Group Resources*. Berne, CH: Haupt. ISBN 3-258-05165-8.

Rockwell, S (1995). *Tough to Reach, Tough to Teach: Students with Behaviour Problems*. Reston, VA: CEC Catalog, The Council for Exceptional Children. ISBN 0-86586-235-4.

Sewell, K (1998). *Breakthroughs: How to Reach Students with Autism*. Reston, VA: CEC Catalog, The Council for Exceptional Children. ISBN 1-57861-060-5.

Gifted and Talented

Bloom, B (ed.)(983). *Developing Talent In Young People* New York: Ballantine Books. ISBN 0-345-31509-X.

Callahan, C (1999). Independent Study: Does It work? *Teaching for high potential*. NAGC, 1 (1) April, 2- 3

Center for Talented Youth-CTY (1994). *Educational Resources for Academically Talented Adolescents*. Baltimore: CTY Publications and Resources, John Hopkins University.

Csikszentmihalyi, M, Rathunde, K R, & Whalen, S (1993). *Talented Teenagers: The Roots of Success & Failure*. New York: Press Syndicate of the University of Cambridge. ISBN 0-521-41578-0.

Doherty, E & Evens, J (1998). *Primary Independent Study – Grades 1-4 and Primary Independent Study Student Book*. Synergetics, P.O. Box 84, East Windsor Hill, Connecticut, 06028. ISBN 0-945984-06-5.

Doherty, E & Evans, J (1989). *Self-Starter Kit for Independent Study – Grades 4-8*. Synergetics, P.O. Box 84, East Windsor Hill, Connecticut 06028. ISBN 0-945984-00-6.

Durden, W & Tangherlini, A (1994). *Smart Kids – How Academic Talents Are Developed and Nurtured in America*. Hogrefe and Huber Publishers, P.O. Box 2487, Kirkland, WA, 98083-2487. ISBN 0-88937-112-1.

Feldhusen, J, Van Tassel-Baska, J & Seeley, K (eds.) (1989). *Excellence in Educating the Gifted*. Denver: Love Publishing Company. ISBN 0-89108-205-0.

Feldhusen, J & Wood, B (1997). Developing Growth Plans for Gifted Students. *GIFTED CHILD TODAY*, November/December, p24-48.

Heller, K, Mönks, F, Sternberg, R J & Subotnik, R (2001). *International Handbook of Giftedness and Talent*. Elsevier Science. ISBN 0 08 043796 6. 2 February 2002.

Kaplan, S (1999). A Learning Centre Approach to Independent Study. *Teaching for high potential*. NAGC, 1 (1) April, p1,2.

Leyden, S (1998). *Supporting the Child of Exceptional Ability*. NACE/Fulton Publication, David Fulton Publishers Ltd., London, England, ISBN 1-85346-516-X.

National Research Centre on Gifted and Talented Children, Salley M Reis, Director, Neag School of Education, University of Connecticut, <http://www.gifted.ucon.edu>

Reis, S, Burns, D & Renzulli, J (1990). *Curriculum Compacting: A Guide for Teachers*. Creative Learning Press Inc., P.O. Box 320 Mansfield Centre, Connecticut 06250.

Renzulli, J (1998). A Rising Tide Lifts All Ships: Developing the Gifts and Talents of All Students. *PHI DELTA KAPPAN*, October, p105-111.

Renzulli, J & Reis, S (1985). *The Schoolwide Enrichment Model: A Comprehensive Plan for Educational Excellence*. Creative Learning Press, Inc., P.O. Box 320, Mansfield Centre, Connecticut 06250. ISBN 0-936386-34-7.

Starko, A.J. & Schack, G.D. (1992). *Looking for data in all the right places:A guidebook for conducting original research with young investigators*. Mansfield Centre, CT: Creative Learning Press, Inc.

Tomlinson, C & Imbeau, M (1999). Teacher to Teacher: Making Independent Study Work. *Teaching for high potential*. NAGC, 1 (1) April p1,4.

Vail, P (1987). *Smart Kids with School Problems: Things to Know and Ways to Help*. London: Penguin Books.

Winner, E (1996). *Gifted Children: Myths and Realities*. Basic Books, 10 East 53rd St., New York, NY 10022-5299. ISBN 0-465-01760-6.

Gifted underachiever

Baum, S.M., Renzulli, J.S., & Herbert, T.P. (1995b). Reversing underachievement: Creative productivity as a systematic intervention. *Gifted Child Quarterly*, 39 (4), 224-235.

Colangelo, N., Kerr, B., Christensen, P. & Maxey, J. (1993). A comparison of gifted underachievers and gifted high achievers. *Gifted Child Quarterly*, 37, 155-160.

Emerick, L. J. (1992). Academic underachievement among the gifted: Students' perceptions of factors that reverse the pattern. *Gifted Child Quarterly*, 36, 140-146.

Lukasic, M., Gorski, V., Lea, M., & Culross, R. (1992). *Underachievement among gifted/talented students: What we really know.* Houston, TX: University of Houston-Clear Lake.

McCall, R. B., Evahn, C., & Kratzer, L. (1992). *High school underachievers: What do they achieve as adults?* Newbury Park, CA: SAGE Publications.

Redding, R.E. (1990). Learning preferences and skill patterns among underachieving gifted adolsecents. *Gifted Child Quarterly*, 34, 72-75.

Reis, S. M., Hebert, T.P., Diaz, E. I., Maxfield, L.R., & Ratley, M.E. (1995). *Case studies of talented students who achieve and underachieve in an urban high school.* Research Monograph 95114, Storrs, CT: University of Connecticut, The National Research Centre for the Gifted and Talented.

Reis, S.M., McCoach, D. B. (2000). 'The underachievement of gifted students – What do we know and where do we go?' *Gifted Child Quarterly*, 44 (3), 152-170.

Renzulli, J.S. & Reis, S. M. (1997). *The schoolwide enrichment model: A comprehensive plan for educational excellence* (2nd ed.). Mansfield Centre, CT: Creative Learning Press.

Rimm, S. (1984). Underachievement … or if God had meant gifted children to run our homes, she would have created them bigger. *Gifted Child Quarterly*. 31, 26-29.

Rimm, S. (1997). An underachievement epidemic. *Educational Leadership,* 54 (7), 18-22.

Supplee, P. l., (1990). Reaching the gufted underachiever. New York: Teacher's College Press.

Whitmore, J. R. (1980). *Giftedness, conflict, and underachievement.* Boston: Allen & Bacon.

Gifted/Learning Disabled

Baum, S M, Owen, S V, & Dixon, J (1991). *To Be Gifted and Learning Disabled: From Identification to Practical Intervention Strategies.* Mansfield Centre, CT: Creative Learning Press.

Daniels, P (983). *Teaching The Gifted/Learning Disabled Child.* Aspen Systems Corporation, 1600 Research Boulevard, Rockville, Maryland 20850, ISBN 0-89443-928-6.

Gerber, P & Ginsberg, R (1990). *Identifying Alterable Patterns of Success in Highly Successful Adults with Learning Disabilities:* Executive summary. Washington, DC: US Department of Education, Educational Information Centre. ERIC Document No. ED342-168.

Gersten, R, Baker, S & Marks, S (1999). *Teaching English-Language Learners with Learning Difficulties: Guiding Principles and Examples from Research-Based Practice*. Reston, VA: CEC Catalog, The Council for Exceptional Children.
ISBN 0-86586-331-8

Olenchak, F (1995). Effects of Enrichment on Gifted/Learning-Disabled Students. Journal for the Education of the Gifted, 18 (4) p385-399.

Reis, S, Neu, T, & McGuire (1997). Case Studies of High Ability Students with Learning Disabilities Who Have Achieved. *Exceptional Children,* 63 (4), p1-12.

Whitmore, J R & Maker, C J (1985). *Intellectual Giftedness in Disabled Persons*. Rockville, MD: Aspen.

Interest Inventories

Kettle, K, Renzulli, J, & Rizza (1998). My Way…An Expression Style Inventory. *Gifted Child Quarterly*, 42 (1), Winter.

Renzulli, J (1977). The Interest-A-Lyzer. Mansfield Centre, CT: Creative Learning Press.

Journals

British Journal of Special Education: A Journal of The National Association for Special Educational Needs. NASEN House, 4/5 Amber Business Village Amber Close, Amington Tamworth, Staffs, B77 4RP, England.

Gifted Child Quarterly. National Association for Gifted Children (NAGC), 1707 L Street, NW, Suite 550, Washington, DC 20036.

EXCEPTIONAL CHILDREN, The Council for Exceptional Children, 1920 Association Drive, Reston, VA, 20191-1589.

European Council for High Ability (ECHA). Dr. Harald Wagner, Bildung und Begabung e.V., Postfach 200201, D-53132 Bonn, Germany. 25 April 2002. info@bildung-und-begabung.de <http://www.echa.ws >

ImaGiNe… Opportunities and Resources for Academically Talented Youth. CTY. Baltimore, Maryland: The Johns Hopkins University.

IS-International School. The ECIS Magazine-To Promote Excellence of Education in International Schools. Suffolk, England: John Catt Educational Ltd.

Journal of Research in International Education. Published in association with the International Baccalaureate Organisation, Jeff Thompson ed. London: SAGE Publications. 6 June 2002. http://www.sagepub.co.uk

Journal of Learning Disabilities, PRO-ED, 8700 Shoal Creek Boulevard, Austin, TX 78757.

Parenting for High Potential: Developing your child's gifts & talents. National Association for Gifted Children, 1707 L. Street, NW, Suite 550, Washington, DC 20036.

TEACHING Exceptional Children. The Council for Exceptional Children, 1920 Association Drive, Reston, VA 20191-1589.

Learning Disabilities

Brock, C & Griffin, R (eds.) (2000). *International Perspectives on Special Educational Needs.* Suffolk, England: John Catt Educational Ltd. ISBN 0 901577 45 6.

Carnell, E & Lodge, C (2001). *Supporting Learning in School: Learning At All Levels in Secondary Schools.* London: SAGE Publications. ISBN 0-7619-7047-9.

Chinn, S & Ashcroft, R (1998). *Mathematics for Dyslexics: A Teaching Handbook* (2nd ed.). London: Whurr Publishers Ltd. ISBN 1 86156 043 5.

Culshaw, C & Walters, D (1988). *Headwork.* Oxford University Press.

Cunningham, C & Davis, H (1988). *Working with Parents: Frameworks for Collaboration,* Children with Special Needs. Open University Educational Enterprises Limited, Milton Keynes, England. ISBN 0-335-15036-7.

Duffy, J (1974). *Type It: A Linguistically Oriented Typing Program.* Educators Publishing Service, 75 Moulton St., Cambridge, MA 02238, ISBN 0-8388-2345-3.

El-Naggar, O (1996). *Specific Learning Difficulties in Mathematics: A Classroom Approach.* NASEN publication. ISBN 0-906730-81-3.

Green, C & Chee, K (1997). *Understanding ADD (Attention Deficit Disorder): A Book for Parents, Teachers and Professionals.* Vermilion Pub. ISBN 0 091817005.

Henderson, A & Miles, E (2001). *Basic Topics in Mathematics for Dyslexics.* London: Whurr Publishers. ISBN 1 86156 211 X.

Hornsby, B (1996). *Before Alpha – Learning Games for the Under Fives.* London: Souvenir Press Ltd.

Hornsby, B (1996). *Overcoming Dyslexia (3rd ed).* New York: Random House.

Hornsby, B & Shear, F (1993). *Alpha to Omega – The A-Z of Teaching Reading, Writing and Spelling.* Portsmouth, NH: Heinemann Educational.

Johnson, K & Bayrd, P (1982). *Megawords, Multisyllabic Words for Reading, Spelling and Vocabulary.* Educators Publishing Service, Inc. 31 Smith Place Cambridge, MA, 02138-1089.

Levine, M (1993). *Developmental Variation and Learning Disorders.* Cambridge, MA: Educators Publishing Service, Inc. ISBN 0-8388-1992-3.

Levine, M (2000) *Educational Care: A System for Understanding and Helping Children with Learning Problems At Home and in School.* Educators Publishing Service, Inc. 31 Smith Place Cambridge, Massachusetts 02138-1089. EPS. 2 February 2002. <http://www.epsbooks.com>

Lindamood-Bell *Visualisation and Verbalisation.* Gander Educational Publications, 412 Higuera Street, Suite 200, San Louis Obispo, CA 93401.

LIPS: Lindamood Phoneme Sequencing. Gander Educational Publications, 412 Higuera Street, Suite 200, San Louis Obispo, CA 93401.

McCarney, S & Bauer, A (1991). *The Parent's Guide to Learning Disabilities: Helping Your LD Child Succeed at Home and School*. Columbia, MO: Hawthorne Educational Services, Inc. ISBN 0-00-000011-6.

Montgomery, D (1998). *Developmental Spelling: A Handbook of Over 100 Spelling Lessons and 50 Different Learning Strategies*. Essex, England: Learning Difficulties Research Project.

Montgomery, D (1997). Spelling: Remedial Strategies. Dorset, England: Cassell. ISBN 0 304 32972 X.

Ott, P (1997). *How to Detect and Manage Dyslexia: A Reference and Resource Manual*. Oxford: Heinemann Educational Publishers. ISBN 0 435 104195.

Peer, L & Reid, G (2001). *Dyslexia: Successful Inclusion in the Secondary School*. London: Fulton.

Peer, L & Reid, G (eds.) (2000). *Multilingualism, Literacy and Dyslexia: A Challenge for Educators*. London: David Fulton Publishers Ltd. ISBN 1-85346-696-4.

Phonic Reference File. Cotterell, G. This file contains Diagnostic Spelling Tests, a Checklist of Basic Sounds and Accompanying lists of words, alphabetically indexed and phonically graded, along with a suggested teaching approach contained in this introduction. The material can be used throughout the age range up to university level. ISBN 185503-196-5.

Pollock, J & Waller, E (1995). *Day-To-Day Dyslexia In The Classroom*. London: Routledge. ISBN 0-415-11132-3.

QRI.3: Qualitative Reading Inventory. Reading, MA: Addison-Wesley Publishing Company.

Ramsden, M. (1999), *The teachers tool box for sound spelling: User's self-training manual, Limited Edition*. Eynesse, France: Melvyn Ramsden. <http://www.members.tripod.com/-MelvynR/>

Sanson, J (200). *What Teachers Can Do – What Schools Can Do – What Learners Can Do – What Parents Can Do*. Sections of Guide to Language Shock, Dyslexia Across Cultures: Multimedia Pack Video. <http://www.ditt-online.org>

Sharp, S. *Handy Hints on Supporting Dyslexia in the Classroom*. <http:www.dyslexic.com/teachtips.htm>

Shaywitz, S. (2003). *Overcoming Dyslexia: A New and Complete Science-Based Program for Overcoming Reading Problems at Any Level*. New York: Alfred A. Knopf. ISBN 0375400125.

Smith, S (1981). *No Easy Answers: The Learning Disabled Child At Home and At School Bantam Book*, Winthrop Publishers, Cambridge, Mass, ISBN 0 533 14138 4.

Smith, S (1992). *Succeeding Against the Odds: Strategies and Insights from the Learning Disabled*. Los Angeles, California: Jeremy P. Tarcher, Inc. ISBN 0-87477-674-0.

Smith, S (2001). *The Power of the Arts: Creative Strategies for Teaching Exceptional Learners*. Baltimore, Maryland: Paul H. Brookes Publishing Co. ISBN 1-55766-484-6.

S.P.I.R.E.: Specialised Program Individualizing Reading Excellence. Kennebunk, Maine: Progress Learning, Inc.

Steck Vaughn Critical Thinking Series (1993). Steck-Vaughn Publishers Co., Austin, Texas.

Strichert, S. (1984). *College and the LD Student*. New York: Grune & Stratton, Inc.

Stirling, E G (1990). *WHICH IS WITCH?* Checklist of Homophones Resources Sales. Helen Arkell Dyslexia Centre, Frensham, Farnham, Surrey GU 10 3BW, United Kingdom.

Teaching Learning Strategies and Study Skills to Students with Learning Disabilities, Attention Deficit Disorders or Special Needs (2001). Boston: Allyn & Bacon, ISBN 0 205335136.

The Wilson Reading System. 175 West Main Street, Millbury, MA 01527-1441. Telephone: 001-508-865-5699, Fax: 001-508-865-9644.

Thompson, M (ed) (2003). *Dyslexic Included – A Whole School Approach*. London: Fulton. ISBN 1-84312-002-X

Thomson, M & Watkins, B (1998). *Dyslexia: A Teaching Handbook (2nd ed.)*. London: Whurr Publishers Ltd. ISBN 1-86156-039-7.

Tokuhama-Espinosa, T (2000). *Raising Multilingual Children: Foreign Language Acquisition and Children*. London: Westport Publications Ltd. ISBN 0-89789-750-1.

Type To Learn: A Phonetic Based Computer Typing Program. Pleasantville, New York: Sunburst/Wings Communications.

Units of Sound – Audio-visual CD ROM. London: The Dyslexia Institute, LDA.

Word Shark 3 – 30 Games for Word Recognition & Spelling. White Space Publishers.

Newsletters

newsletter@allkindsofminds.org Newsletter from Dr Mel Levine's All Kinds of Minds institute, US.

Schwab Learning Foundation. 10 June 2002. <http:www.SchwabLearning.org>

Shortcuts – A free newsletter published monthly, which provides information and links on current educational issues, Jennifer Henley and Anne Poenisch Publishers, subscribe at: Henley & Poenisch. 9 October 2001. <shortcuts@international-ed.com>

Organisations

British Dyslexia Association, 98 London Road, Reading, RG1 5AU, UK

CHADD: Children and Adults with Attention Deficit Hyperactivity Disorder. 8181 Professional Place, Suite 201, Landover, MD 20785. Telephone: 1-800-233-4050. 11 June 2002. URL <http://www.chad.org>

National Association for Able Children in Education (NAGC). Westminster College, Oxford, 0X29AT, England. NAGC. 7 February 2002. nace@ox-west.ac.uk <http://www.ox-west.ac.uk/nace/>

National Association for Gifted Children, 1707 L Street, NW, Suite 550, Washington, DC 20036.

National Centre for Learning Disabilities (NCLD). 11 June 2002. <http://www.ncld.org/>

The Council for Exceptional Children, 1920 Association Drive, Reston, Virginia 20191-1589.

Publications

Centre for Talented Youth (CTY) Publications and Resources. The Johns Hopkins University, 3400 N. Charles St. Baltimore, Maryland, USA 21218.

Creative Learning Press, Inc. Educational Resources. P.O.Box 320, Mansfield Centre, CT 06250, Tel: 001-888-518-8004, Fax: 001-860-429-8118, <www.creativelearningpress.com>.

Education: Books & Journals. London: Paul Chapman Publishing, A SAGE Publications Company. 6 June 02. <http://www.PaulChapmanPublishing.co.uk>

Gornik, M, McFiggen, D, Peters, H & Rowan, M (1993). *How to Live 'Til Friday: Practical Teaching Strategies for all Classroom Models*. Cleveland, Ohio: Friday Associates.

Hayden, M & Thompson, J (1998). International Education: Principles and Practice. London: Kogan Page Ltd. ISBN 0 74942694 2.

Kusuma-Powell, O & Powell, W. (eds.) (2000). Count Me In! – Developing Inclusive International Schools. Overseas Schools Advisory Council, Department of State, Washington, DC 20522-0132.

Jamestown Publishers: A division of NTC/Contemporary Publishing Co. Special Education. 4255 West Touhy Avenue, Lincolnwood, Illinois 60646-1975 <http://www.jamestownpublishers.com>

National Association for Gifted Children (NAGC) Publications List, Winter 2002, 1707 L Street, NW, Suite 550, Washington, DC 20036. NAGC. Winter 2002. <http://www.nagc.org>

National Professional Resources, Inc., *Best Sellers, Spring 2001: Video & Print Resources*, Total Talent Portfolio: A Systematic Plan to Identify and Nuture Gifts and Talents, p 15.

Optimal Match Publications and Resources. Advisory Committee on Exceptional Children and Youth, Office of Overseas Schools, US Department of State, Washington, D.C. 20520 and Centre for Talented Youth, The Johns Hopkins University, 3400 N. Charles St. Baltimore, Maryland, USA 21218.

PRO-ED, Catalogue of Educational Materials and Tests, 8700 Shoal Creek Blvd., Austin, TX 78757-6897, Tel: 001-512-451-3246, Fax: 001-512-451-8542.

Synergetics: Differentiating Instruction for All Students. P.O. Box 84, East Windsor Hill, CT 06028-0084 <http://www.synergeticspress.com>

Testing

Educational Records Bureau Comprehensive Testing Program, IV edition, 220 E. 42nd St.

Suite 100, New York, New York 10017. Telephone: 1-800-989-372. ERB. 25 April 2002. <http://www.erbtest.org>

Secondary Level English Proficiency (SLEP), ETS (1997),<http://www.ets.org>

Silver, S A & Clampit, M K (1990). WISC-R Profiles of High Ability Children: Interpretation of Verbal-Performance Discrepancies. *Gifted Child Quarterly*, 34 (2) p76-79.

Test of Written Language-3. Pro-Ed, 8700 Shoal Creek Boulevard, Austen, Texas, 78757-6897.

Truch, S (1993). *The WISC-III Companion: A guide to Interpretation and Educational Intervention*. Pro-Ed, 8700 Shoal Creek Boulevard, Austin, Texas, 78757-6897. ISBN 0-89079-585-1.

Training Programmes

All Kinds of Minds Institute: A Non-Profit Institute for the Understanding of Differences in Learning, Dr. Mel Levine, Founder and Co-Chair, University of North Carolina, Chapel Hill, Summer Course in Neurodevelopmental Variation for Clinicians and Education Professionals. For more information log on to Dr. Melvin Levine, 19 April 2002. <http://www.allkindsofminds.org >

Confratute — a yearly summer intensive on enrichment teaching and learning. Confratute is a combined CONFerence, FRATernity and InstiTUTE geared toward providing educators with strategies for enrichment teaching and learning. This programme is highly relevant for educators at international schools. Share your interest in enrichment teaching and learning, talent development and gifted education with educators and experts from throughout the United States and several overseas nations. Every year in July, attendance possible for one or two weeks. More information please see <www.gifted.uconn.edu> or fax: 001-860-486-2900.

Hornsby Diploma: Distance Learning Course in Specific Learning Difficulties, Hornsby International Dyslexia Centre, Glenshee Lodge, 261 Trinity Road, London SW18 3SN, England. Telephone: 44-(0)181-877-3539, Secretary. 7 February 2002. <courses@hornsby.demon.co.uk>

Optimal Match Network Institute (OMNI), The Johns Hopkins University, Baltimore, Maryland. Strands include: Introduction to Diagnostics, Classroom Strategies for Teaching the Highly Able, Theory of Language Acquisition and Strategies of English as a Second Language in the Classroom, and Classroom Strategies for the LD Student. To apply for summer courses, write to: Association of American Schools in South America, 14750 N.W. 77th Court, Suite 210, Miami Lakes, Fl 33016, US. Telephone: 001-305-821-0345.

Opportunities for advanced training in gifted education for MA, Advanced Diploma and non-degree students

The University of Connecticut offers a Master's or Advanced Diploma Programme with the following features:

- A choice of six different graduate courses each summer.
- Attendance at two summer conferences on the Storrs campus.
- NCATE accreditation.
- Three-four weeks on UConn campus for each of Three Summers.
- Distance Learning courses (via mail and e-mail) during Fall and Spring semesters.
- Strategy-based courses that apply high-end learning techniques to school improvement initiatives.
- Continuous faculty-student communication, advisement and mentoring via on-site conferences and e-mail correspondence.

For more information about The National Research Center on the Gifted and Talented at the University of Connecticut, please visit 28 April 2002. <http://www.gifted.uconn.edu>. For more information on the advanced training, please e-mail: dsiegle@uconn.edu. *Inquire also about the convenient distance learning opportunities.*

For information on partly online *German language advanced training* in cooperation with the University of Connecticut, please visit Stedtnitz. 28 April 2002. <http://www.stedtnitz.ch > or www.semeuropa.org, or e-mail stedtnitz@bluewin.ch. In Switzerland, Dr Ulrike Stedtnitz and Dr Monika Brunsting offer a two-year professional training programme on enrichment teaching and learning. For more information, see <www.stedtnitz.ch> or e-mail: stedtnitz@bluewin.ch.

University of Bath, UK. School of Education, Centre for the Study of Education in an International Context offers to teachers who want to continue their professional training a Distance Learning Masters and Doctorate degrees. Over 500 international teachers attend the summer courses and continue during the school year with the Distance Learning programme with their tutors by fax, e-mail and can continue at local study centers at Amnan, Bangkok, Buenos Aires, Mauritius and Yokohama as well as the main study centre at Bath. For more information, contact Director of Admissions, Claverton Down, Bath BA2 7AY, UK. Tel: +44-1225-826-826, Fax: +44 1225 826366 or URL http://www.bath.ac.uk

Videos

Celebrating Gifts & Talents, National Association for Gifted Children, 1707 L. Street, Suite 550, Washington, DC 20036.

Effective Teaching for Dyslexic/All College Students, Centre for the Advancement of College Teaching, P.O. Box 1867, Brown University, Providence, RI 02912.

ERIC Database of Videos in Special and Gifted Education (VISAGE). CEC Publication Sales, VISAGE Database number R5090. Council for Exceptional Children, 1920 Association Drive, Reston, Virginia, USA 22091-1589.

How Difficult Can This Be (F.A.T. City Workshop), Richard Lavoie, PBS Video, 1320 Br addock Place, Alexandria, Virginia 22314-1698 <http://Idonline.org/Id_store/Idproject.html>

Language Shock-Dyslexia Across Cultures: Multimedia Training Pack (1999). European Children in Crisis for Children with Learning Difficulties (ECIC). 1 rue Defacqz, R-1000 Brussels, Belgium. Telephone/Fax: +32-2-537-4836.

Learning Disabilities and Social Skills: Last One Picked...First One Picked On, Richard Lavoie, PBS Video, 1320 Braddock Place, Alexandria, Virginia 22314-1698.

Project HIGH HOPES: Discovering and Developing Talent in Students with Special Needs, A Javits Act Program R206R00001, ACES – 205 Skiff St, Hamden, CT 06517.

Websites and e-mail addresses

ADD/ADHD Online Resource and Support: http://www.adders.org

DLK Toolset, Literacy and Mathswork. 6 June 2002. <http://www.dlk.co.uk>

<http://www.elsevier.com/locate/giftedness>

ERIC Clearinghouse on Disabilities and Gifted Education. 6 June 02. ericec@cec.sped.org or telephone 001-703-264-9475.

Distance Learning: A thorough overview of distance learning programmes can be found at: http://www.hoagiesgifted.org/distance_learning.htm/

Gifted and Talented (TAG) Resources Home Page. Contains links to resources, enrichment programs, talent searches, summer programs, mailing lists. 6 June 2002. <http://www.gifted + resources >

K-12 100 Best Curriculum Resources. 7 February 2002. <http://www.lone-eagles.com/curric.html>

National Attention Deficit Disorder Association, Highland Park, Il, USA. <http://www.add.org>

Read Naturally – Fluency, Rate & Comprehension program using audiotapes of CD ROM. Read Naturally. 2 February 2002. <http://www.readnaturally.com>

Rewards program-Reading Excellence, Word Attack, & Root Development Strategies. Sopris West Publishers. 2 February 2002. <http://www.sopriswest.com>

Schwab Learning Foundation: Helping kids with differences be successful in learning and life (2000). *A Guide to differences & disabilities in learning*. Order free materials online. SchwabLearning. 7 February 2002. <http://www.SchwabLearning.org>

Schwab Learning Foundation: Helping kids with differences be successful in learning and life (2001). *A Parent's Guide to differences & disabilities in learning.* Order free materials online. SchwabLearning. 2 February 2002.
<http://www.SchwabLearning.org>

Schwab Learning Foundation: Helping kids with differences be successful in learning and life (1999). *Bridges To Reading, What To Do When You Suspect Your Child Has A Reading Problem: A Kit of First-Step Strategies.* Order free materials online. SchwabLearning. 7 February 2002. <http://www.SchwabLearning.org>

Schwab Learning Foundation: Helping kids with earning differences be successful in learning and life (2001). *Educator's Guide to Learning Differences.* Order online for free materials. SchwabLearning. 2 February 2002.
<http://www.SchwabLearning.org>

Schwab Learning Foundation. *TeachEach: Classroom Strategies to Teach and Reach All Learners.* 7 February 2002. <http://www.schwablearning.org>

Snyder, T (1998). *Great Teaching with the Internet Resource Guide.* Watertown, MA: Tom Snyder Productions, Inc. Telephone:1-800-342-0236, Fax: 011-617-926-6222. ISBN YMA XINT SEM U 01

Teens Helping Teens: A Web page designed by dyslexic teens to help teens (and others). <http://www.Idteens.org>

textHELP Systems Ltd. 28 April 2002. info@texthelp.com <http://texthelp.com>

The Learning Toolbox. This Website is designed to assist secondary students with learning disabilities and ADHD to become more effective learners using research-based strategies. The Learning Toolbox is designed for independent use by students, special and general education teachers, and parents. http://coe.jmu.edu/Learningtoolbox/ Training of Cognitive Strategies. 28 April 2002. <http://pedcurmac13.unifr.ch/CogStrat.html>

Appendix F

Bibliography

Adda, A (1999). *Le livre de l'enfant doué*. Paris: Editions Solar.

Advisory Committee on Exceptional Children and Youth (ACECY-IAAY/JHU) (1997). <http://www.jhu/-gifted/acecy/acey.htm> Baltimore, Maryland: The Johns Hopkins University.

Advisory on Exceptional Children and Youth (ACECY)(1993). *The Optimal Match Concept: Putting the Pieces Together for the Exceptional student in American Overseas Schools*. Washington, DC: Office of Overseas schools, US Department of State.

American Psychological Association Diagnostic and Statistics Manual (1994). Washington DC: American Psychological Press Inc.

Bartlett, K (1995). *Internationalism: Getting Beneath the Surface, Part 2 – The Role of Language*. International Schools Curriculum Project. Vienna: Vienna International School.

Brock, C & Griffin, R (eds.) (2000) *International Perspectives on Special Educational Needs*. p191. Suffolk: John Catt Educational Limited

Centre for Talented Youth-CTY Annual Report (2000). *Ideal Teacher of Gifted Children*, p15. Maryland: CTY.

Centre for Talented Youth-CTY (1994). *The Optimal Match: A Primer for Change*. Centre for Talented Youth, Baltimore, Maryland: The John Hopkins University.

Chinn, S & Ashcroft, R (1998). *Mathematics for Dyslexics: A Teaching Handbook (2nd ed.)*. London: Whurr Publishers Ltd.

Cohen, R (1987). *When the Words Are There But the Hand Won't Write*. International Herald Tribune, Washington Post Writers Group, June 12.

Communique (1998) *Students with Concomitant Gifts and Learning Disabilities*, New NAGC Position Paper, Washington DC, December, p12.

Cooper, C (1998). *Integrating Gifted Education into the Total School Curriculum: Practical Tips for Administrators*. Hamburg: ECIS Conference.

Daniels, H (ed.) (1996). *An Introduction to Vygotsky*. London: Routledge Publishers.

Diagnostic and Statistics Manual (fourth ed.) (1994). American Psychiatric Association, Washington, DC: American Psychiatric Press, Inc.

Durden, W G (1998). *Points to Consider When Forwarding Initiatives for Highly Capable Students in American-Sponsored Overseas Schools*. Advisory Committee for Exceptional

Children and Youth, Washington DC: Office of Overseas Schools, US Department of State.

Durden, W G (1996). *Status Questionnaire*. Advisory Committee on Exceptional Children and Youth, Washington, DC: Office of Overseas Schools, US Department of State.

Durden, W G & Mills, C J (1996). *Position paper: The Optimal Match-The Middle Path toward the Renewal of Education*, p1-5. Baltimore, Maryland: IAAY, The Johns Hopkins University.

Durden, W G & Tangherlini, AE (1993). *Smart Kids – How Academic Talents are Developed and Nurtured in America*. Kirkland, WA: Hogrefe and Huber Publishers.

Educational Resources for Academically Talented Adolescents (1994). Centre for Talented Youth (CTY). Baltimore: Publications and Resources, The Johns Hopkins University.

European Council of International Schools (1997). *School Evaluation and Accreditation, a Professionally Recognised Programme for the Improvement of International Schools World-Wide*. Petersfield, England: European Council of International Schools.

Feldhusen, J, Van Tassel-Baska, J, & Seeley, K (1989). *Excellence in Educating the Gifted*, p4. Denver Colorado: Love Publishing Company.

Gallagher, J (1989). *Educating Exceptional Children*, p401. Boston, MA: Houghton Mifflin Company.

Goldman, L, Genel, M, Bezman, R, & Slanetez, P. (1998). Diagnosis and Treatment of Attention-Deficit/Hyperactivity Disorder in Children and Adolescents: Council Report. *Journal of American Medical Association*, 279 (14), p1100-1107.

Haldimann, M (1999). Spatial Ability and the Academic Success of Sixth Grade Students at International Schools. *International Schools Journal*, XVIII (2), p48-57.

Haldimann, M (1998). Special Learning Needs in International Schools: The Optimal Match Concept (1998). in *International Education Principles and Practice*. Hayden, M & Thompson, J (eds.), p133-145. London: Kogan Page Limited.

Hollington, A (1994). A Very Special International Education. *International Schools Journal*, 27, p27-30.

Johns Hopkins University Centre for Talented Youth (2000) *Annual Report*. CTY, The Johns Hopkins University, 3400 North Charles Street, Baltimore, MD 21218 ctyinfo@jhu.edu

Kusuma-Powell, O & Powell, W (eds.) (2000). *Count Me In! Developing Inclusive International Schools*. Overseas Schools Advisory Council, Department of State, Washington, DC 20522-0132.

Lerner, J (1988). *Learning Disabilities: Theories, Diagnosis, and Teaching Strategies (fifth ed.)*, p8. Boston, MA: Houghton Mifflin Company.

Levine, M (1988). *The Concentration Cockpit: Guidelines for its Utilization – Explaining Attention Deficits to Children*. Cambridge: Educators Publishing Service, Inc.

McCoach, D B & Siegle, D (2003). Factors That Differentiate Underachieving Gifted Students From High-Achieving Gifted Students. *Gifted Child Quarterly*, 47 (2) Spring, p144-154.

Marland, S P (1972). *Education of the gifted and talented.* (Report to the Subcommittee on Education, Committee on Labor and Public Welfare, US Senate). Washington, DC: US Government Printed Office.

Miller, C J & Castellanos, F X (1998) Attention Deficit/Hyperactivity Disorders. *Pediatrics in Review*, 19 (11) November, p373-384.

Mills, C J & Durden, W G (1996). Standardised Tests: Still an Essential Option for International Schools. *The International Educator*, X (4), A/M, p1,6.

National Association of Gifted Children (1998). *Children with Gifts and Learning Disabilities*, p12.

National Research Centre on Gifted and Talented Children (2002). *Increasing Academic Achievement Study.* University of Connecticut: Neag School of Education.

New Mexico Learning Disabilities Association (NMLDA) (1998). *What Are Learning Disabilities?* 6301 Menaul Blvd, Albuquerque, New Mexico, 87110-3323.

Percy, G (2003). *CIS/NEASC Standards and Indicators from the Guide to School Evaluation and Accreditation* (Seventh Edition). CIS Accreditation Committee. Spain: CIS.

Pfiffner, L (1996). *All About ADHD: The Complete Practical Guide for Classroom Teachers,* p164. New York: Scholastic Professional Books.

Reis, S (2000). Gifted Students with Learning Disabilities. *Communique.* Washington, DC: National Association for Gifted Children.

Reis, S (2000). The Underachievement of Gifted Students: Multiple Frustrations and Few Solutions. *Promise: New Jersey Association for Gifted Children*, 8 (3), p4-16.

Reis, S, Burns, D, & Renzulli, J (1990). *Curriculum Compacting: A Guide for Teachers*. Connecticut: Creative Learning Press, Mansfield Centre.

Reis, S. M., McGuire, J. M., & Neu, T. W. (2000). Compensation strategies used by high ability students with learning disabilities who succeed in college. *Gifted Child Quarterly*, 44(2), 123-134.

Renzulli, J & Reis, S (1986). Overview of the Schoolwide Enrichment Model in A *Comprehensive System for Educating the Gifted & Talented.* Missouri: Creative Workshop Associates.

Renzulli, J. S., & Reis, S. M. (1994). Research related to the Schoolwide Enrichment Triad Model. *Gifted Child Quarterly*, 38(1), 7-20.

Reyes, M de la Luz (1992). Challenging venerable assumptions: Literacy instruction for linguistically different students. *Harvard Educational Review*, 62 (4), p 427-46.

Robin, A (1999). Attention Deficit/Hyperactivity Disorder in Adolescents, Pediatric Clinics of North America, 46 (5), pp 1028-1029.

Shaywitz, S (2003). *Overcoming Dyslexia: A New and Complete Science-Based Program for Overcoming Reading Problems at Any Level*. New York: Alfred A. Knopf.

Siegle, D (2002). *National Study of Underachievers*. National Research Centre on the Gifted and Talented, University of Connecticut, <http:www.gifted.uconn.edu>

Stumpf, H & Haldimann, M (1997). Spatial Ability and Academic Success of Sixth Grade Students at International Schools. *School Psychology International*, 18, p245-259.

Smith, S (1992). *Succeeding Against the Odds: Strategies and Insights from the Learning Disabled*. Los Angeles, California: Jeremy P. Tarcher, Inc.

Smith, S (1998/1999). The Hidden Dimension of Learning: Time and Space, *Their World*, New York: National Council of Learning Disabilities.

Sternberg, R J (2001). Giftedness as Developing Expertise. *High Ability Studies: The Journal of the European Council for High Ability (ECHA)*, 12 (2) p159-178.

Subhi, T (2001). *The Qatari Centre for the Gifted and Talented*. ECHA News, 15 (1) p 3-4.

Tahmincioglu, E (2001). *Incompetent? Please Take a Promotion*. Züirch: International Herald Tribune, Thursday, November 22, 2001.

Tarkin, L. (2002). Early intervention is crucial for autism. *International Herald Tribune*, October 24.

Terrassier, J-C (1998). *Guide practique de l'enfant surdoué*. Paris: Editions ESF.

Thompson, M & Watkins, B (1998). *Dyslexia: A Teaching Handbook*. London: Whurr Publishers Ltd.

TIME (2002). *Inside the World of Autism*, p40-49. Amsterdam: Time Warner Pub. B.V.

Ward, R & Purvis, P (1997). *Twelve Management Tips for Children with ADHD*, Kansas City, Missouri: Behavioural Pediatric Psychology Program at The Children's Mercy Hospital.

Wechsler, D (1991). *Wechsler Intelligence Scale for Children, 3rd edition, manual*, p9. San Antonio, Texas: The Psychological Corporation, Harcourt Brace and Company.

Wilson, D (2003). *SpLD Software*. Equal Opportunities Department, Harton School, Lisle Road, South Shields, NE34 6DL. Email: DavidRitchieWilson@compuserve.com Website: http://www.tomwilson.com/david

Authors' biographies

Martha Haldimann has been involved in international education for 23 years. She has a BS in Elementary Education, an MA in Music Composition and Education, and an MS in Psychology. She was the Educational Psychologist and Learning Support Co-ordinator at the International School of Berne, Switzerland for 20 years. She is currently an Educational Psychologist at the John F. Kennedy International School, Switzerland where she has filled that position for 22 years. Mrs Haldimann is a frequent speaker at international school conferences, and her research on spatial ability in collaboration with Dr. Heinrich Stumpf, Center for Talented Youth, Baltimore, was made possible by an ECIS Fellowship grant.

Angela Hollington received her degree in Special Education from Nottingham University and has worked in international education for 19 years, having taught in England, Austria, Belgium and Switzerland. She was head of the Special Education Unit at the International School of Brussels and set up the Learning Support Department at the International School of Zug, where she was also Early Childhood Principal. She is currently the Principal at the International School of Geneva, Pregny Rigot Campus, a school that has its own Learning Centre and welcomes children who are different.